VIKINGS BOLD:
THEIR VOYAGES
& ADVENTURES

Vikings Bold:
Their Voyages
& Adventures

By Samuel Carter III

Illustrated by Ted Burwell

Thomas Y. Crowell Company · New York

For H. COPLAND ROBINSON III, &
all young people seeking new frontiers

Contents

Introductory Note

~~~~~~~~~~~~~~~~~~~~~~~~

If one were to choose some other age or some other society
to live in, one might well choose to be a Viking. For no
other people on earth enjoyed adventure more or excelled
the Vikings in getting pleasure and excitement out of life.

Every Viking day promised a new adventure. Every
season had its special challenge. Not a year went by when
the chance for discovery or conquest of another land did
not present itself.

The horizons of the Viking world were limitless because
they included the uncharted and infinite surrounding seas.
The Vikings made these seas their own and ruled the waves
for 300 years, as none had done before them.

The Vikings were of extraordinary importance to their times, and they are important to us today. Many Americans' ancestors came from countries the Vikings invaded and sometimes shaped. These sea marauders left their mark almost everywhere in the western world—England, Ireland, France, Spain, Russia, Greece, Arabia, and Africa. They settled in Iceland and Greenland, and discovered America 500 years before Columbus.

Though they conquered and plundered country after country in the Christian world, they helped in time to carry Christianity to the remote corners of the globe. They built cities and established democratic governments in many lands. They awakened Europe from the torpor of the Middle Ages because they challenged its peoples to rise and to fight for their rights and institutions.

It must have been a great age to live in. Life was not easy nor filled with creature comforts. Certainly there often was danger and the need for courage and resourcefulness. But the Vikings had no doubts about the future. They made their own future. Even when at times they failed, and died bravely in defeat, they could count on immortality in that most glorious of pagan heavens, Valhalla. The story of the Vikings is not a simple story with an easy plot. It is made up of many battles, many incidents, and many voyages. Put together they provide a panorama of perhaps the most exciting epoch in man's history, an era that did much to shape the world as it is today.

VIKINGS BOLD:
THEIR VOYAGES
& ADVENTURES

Sea People of the North

If one looks at a map of Europe one sees that the Scandinavian countries—Norway, Sweden, and Denmark—are far north; Norway and Sweden extend beyond the Arctic Circle. Thus the early Scandinavian peoples were far removed from central Europe, where civilization was more advanced and Christianity prevailed.

What were these northern peoples like?

It is apparent from the map that wherever people live in these Scandinavian countries they are not far from the sea. They are almost completely surrounded by long coastlines, with numerous inland lakes and rivers leading to the sea. The coastlines are dented by many sounds and bays and, particularly in Norway, by numerous fjords, which are steep and narrow inlets.

Thus, by circumstance, the Norsemen (or Scandinavians) were sea people. They lived by the sea as fishermen or traveled by the sea as traders. If they farmed the land, raising cattle, sheep, and chickens, they established their farms close to sea or sound so that they could carry their produce to market by boat.

The boundaries of these Scandinavian countries were in Viking days approximately what they are today, allowing for frequent disputes and battles over border territories. There were no great cities. Population was clustered in those areas near the water where a slightly more temperate climate made year-round sea communication possible. Thus, at the beginning of the Viking era, the market towns and trading centers were principally in southern Norway, the Jutland Peninsula of Denmark, and southeastern Sweden.

The Viking age is considered to extend roughly from A.D. 800 to 1100. The word *Viking*, generally accepted as meaning seaborne marauder, probably comes from the Scandinavian word *vic* for bay or inlet. Thus it applied to persons or pirates who lurked along the shores to pounce on passing victims. Or it may come from the ancient Norse word *vig* for battle, or the Latin *vicus* for camp. All these terms, whichever one accepts, suggest men who engaged in conquest and adventure far abroad.

Actually the Norse people had been living on their lands for at least 10,000 years before they became known as Vikings. They were always an orderly people who led hard, well-disciplined lives. The climate was harsh and the times were rough. There were many pirates and highway-

men abroad, so one was never safe without a broadsword
at his side.

The Vikings built their houses solidly of those materials
that were available. Generally they built with logs, using

clay to fill the gaps between the logs. Instead of windows there were slits or peepholes through which they could watch for enemies and fire their arrows if necessary. If there were windows they were covered with stretched animal membranes.

These houses had one large central room, or hall. There was a hearth fire in the center of it, with a hole in the roof to carry off the smoke. Here the family lived and slept and ate. And there was plenty of room for festive get-togethers, for the winter nights were very long, and people often assembled in one another's homes for safety and companionship. They sang, told stories, and played such games as chess and checkers.

Besides working as fishermen and farmers, often as both, the Norsemen practiced many crafts. There were great forests in Norway and Sweden, so the men became skillful lumbermen and carpenters. They built wonderfully designed wooden boats, and their houses and furniture were decorated with beautiful carvings. Their great halls had tables and chairs much like those of today, with a special chair for the master of the house. They built sleds and carts of wood, and also made saddles, for, though the Norsemen depended a great deal on their boats for transportation, they also had horses. They were excellent riders and sometimes took their horses in their ships on overseas expeditions.

They were also skilled metalworkers, for there were iron mines in the northern mountains, and gold and silver were obtained through trade with the countries around

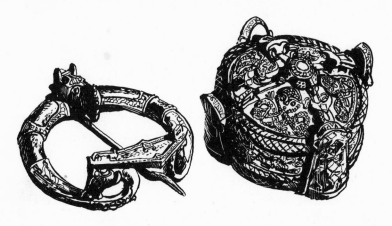

them. They made their own tools and kitchen utensils. Their
weapons were beautifully inlaid with silver and bronze,
and they made jewelry for both men and women. The
Norse loved ornaments, and took great pride in their appearance.

They were stalwart and well built, blond, and blue-
eyed, though the people of Denmark were more brunet
than their neighbors. They were known by descriptive
nicknames such as Thorkell the Tall or Harald Fairhair.
It was as good a way as any of identifying one another.

They made their own clothes. The women wore linen
undergarments and long wool dresses belted at the waist.

Their shoulders and necks were bare for they were proud of their fair complexions. Married women wore their hair up, braided and coiled about their heads. Unmarried women and girls wore their hair extremely long.

The men wore trousers and long shirts of wool. At sea they wore oiled skins as protection against wind and spray. Both men and women wore boots of leather or soft kid, bound to the feet with thongs of walrus hide.

Living in a cold climate and working hard, they ate enormous meals. They had two meals a day, morning and evening. A typical meal might include several kinds of fish, lamb, beef, and pork, with onions and cabbages for vegetables. Rye bread was common, and dairy products such as butter and cheese were made. Honey was used for sweetening, but sweet desserts were rare. Apples, nuts, and berries were their only special treats.

Though the Vikings considered themselves free and independent, they were not all equally free and independent. Their society was divided into distinct classes.

At the bottom level, dressed always in white, were the slaves, or thralls. They were often people who had been captured from the native tribes of Russia, or who were prisoners of war from conquered countries such as Ireland.

Next were the freemen or peasants, who made up the majority of the population. They were the farmers and the fishermen, and they owned land, which meant that they could vote. Above the peasantry was the aristocracy. These were the chiefs and the *jarls*, or earls, the latter sometimes related to the king. An earl often had his own ship and his own band of followers which he would lead into battle in time of war.

Above the aristocracy were the kings. Prior to the Viking period, Scandinavia was divided into numerous small kingdoms, and the term *king* was loosely applied to any leader strong enough to remain in power and control his local subjects. By the start of the Viking age, however, each of the Scandinavian countries—Norway, Sweden, and Denmark—had its own relatively stable dynasty, with the kings succeeded by their sons, or princes.

The form of Norse government varied with the time and place. But in spite of their warlike posture there were few ruthless dictators, for the kings were dependent on the loyalty of earls and chieftains, who in turn ruled through the support of their neighbors. Though individual strength and heroism in battle might end in leadership, the leader was still beholden to his people. There was a sort of natural democracy in the Vikings' political behavior.

The story is told of the Viking crew who arrived in a foreign port and were asked, "Who is your captain?" The reply was, "We have no captain. We are all equal." This generally was the attitude of Vikings on seagoing expeditions or even on the field of battle.

At first perhaps in Denmark and soon in Norway and Sweden, almost every community had its district court or *thing*, in which every freeman had a vote and a voice in the affairs of his locality. The *thing* met regularly to make the laws and settle the disputes. But enforcement of the laws was up to the individual, since there were no police. This meant that people often took matters into their own hands and settled their differences with weapons.

At the start of the Viking era, the Norsemen were pagans, worshiping their own pantheon of gods. Odin was the god of the aristocracy, for he had power over war and warriors. Thor was the god of the common people; he made crops grow and provided fish to catch. These names still survive in the English language. From Odin's Day comes the word *Wednesday* and from Thor's Day, *Thursday*. From a minor god Frey comes the word *Friday*.

Because the Scandinavian countries were remote from the rest of Europe, they did not share in the medieval learning of the time. Viking education, particularly among the aristocracy, was mostly in terms of handicrafts. Young girls learned to sew, weave tapestries, play musical instruments. Young men learned carpentry and ironmongering. At an early age boys learned to ride and to hunt with bow and arrow. They were trained to take up arms when necessary.

The Vikings had no paper to write on. The parchments and papyrus of other countries had not yet reached Scandinavia. But they had their own alphabet of 24 characters, simplified to 16 characters as the Viking age progressed. Each character or *rune* stood for a major sound and sometimes more than one sound, which makes translation difficult. This type of writing was called "rune."

There was a certain secrecy about runic inscriptions, for the majority of people were illiterate. They thought that those who knew and could transcribe the alphabet were in possession of supernatural powers. Someone who could write, a runemaster, was regarded as a sort of magician, and runic inscriptions were regarded as omens of good luck or charms against evil spirits.

The runes were carved on flat pieces of wood or stone. Runic inscriptions are found in many parts of Scandinavia today, and in countries where the Vikings visited. The messages carved were usually very simple: "Sigurd erected this stone in memory of her husband Siegfred who fell at the battle of Svold." Yet even these scant writings tell much about the history of the Norse people.

Another source of information is the *sagas*, which were stories and legends concerning Viking adventures. These

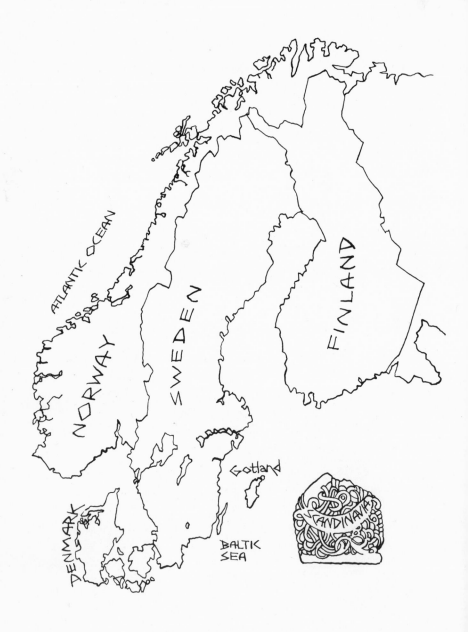

ATLANTIC OCEAN

NORWAY

SWEDEN

FINLAND

Gotland

DENMARK

BALTIC
SEA

SCANDINAVIA

stories were passed down from one generation to another by word of mouth and not actually written down until the twelfth century by monks and scholars hired by wealthy Viking chieftains. The sagas represent a unique monument to the Viking age and a valuable contribution to the literature of the world—purely Viking in their origin, their composition, and their content.

Because the sagas were created to amuse and thrill the audience, they were often elaborated. Exaggerations or romantic incidents would be added with successive tellings. Though not strictly reliable, the sagas do provide much historical data, along with some of the most vivid prose in any language.

Another source of information is the documents found in countries that the Vikings visited and often raided. The plundered monasteries and churches kept records of the Viking raids, written down by the monks. Because these people had been the victims of Viking aggression, their accounts are highly negative and the Vikings are described as little more than ruthless killers.

Ruthless and cruel they often were, but they had other qualities as well. For example, within their own communities the Vikings had a high sense of justice and fair play. Though proud and independent, they were extremely loyal to their own people and their leaders. If they sometimes fought brutally, and killed indiscriminately, it was because they were greatly outnumbered in the countries they invaded. They felt that they could not afford to leave an enemy standing.

But what drove them to other countries in the first place? For one thing, the fertile areas of Norway, Denmark, and Sweden were limited in size. The estates of one man were inherited by his eldest son, forcing any other sons to find land for themselves.

Also, because a freeman was allowed to have several wives, he often had many children. Overpopulation became such a problem that infants were sometimes thrown in the sea or left to die of exposure. The only other cure for overpopulation was to seek new land overseas.

But it was not only land hunger that drove the Vikings abroad. It was, too, the thrill of adventure and the lure of wealth. By the year 800 or before, the Vikings were trading with merchants in England, France, Byzantium (the eastern Roman empire), and even Arabia. They learned that these countries were rich in precious metals and religious ornaments, in silks and gems and spices. The Vikings wanted some of these riches for themselves, and the fame and position that wealth provides.

No doubt for the young men just the lure of adventure was enough to set them roving. The sea was to them what outer space is to the modern world. The lands across the sea were like other planets, begging to be discovered and explored.

Finally, the Norsemen had the ability, by the ninth century at least, to make long ocean voyages over stormy seas. More important than that ability was the spirit and boldness to do so, and the daring to extend their voyages clear across the North Atlantic. Even such venturous seamen as the Arabs and Phoenicians, though they had invented sail much earlier than the Vikings, scarcely dared to trespass far beyond their Mediterranean Sea.

Moreover, the Vikings had learned to build ships far more seaworthy than any people had before them. Their vessels were stout enough to survive harsh Atlantic storms, yet light and maneuverable enough to sweep down rivers and capture a town before the townsfolk knew that they were there.

The time was ripe for the Vikings: the countries around them were rich and often weakly defended. And the Vikings were ripe for the time: impatient with what they had, eager for wealth and glory. These conditions came together and exploded, just as certain chemicals, when properly mixed, will burst into flame.

2

The Viking Character

What was it like to be a Viking? What were *they* like in the way they lived and fought and ranged across the world?

They stand out in history because they exhibited characteristics not common to the medieval world around them —traits that were essential to their nature and survival. Among these qualities were extreme courage and loyalty, skill with arms, individual daring, and the willingness to take great risks and stake their lives upon the outcome. Not only the defense of their farms and property but their success in gaining wealth abroad depended on their military prowess.

The first things a young boy in the Viking countries learned were how to shoot with a bow and arrow, how to wield the sword and axe, how to pierce a target with a spear. Above all he sought the great privilege of going i-viking overseas, which meant participating in a raid on foreign shores. On these amphibious ventures he knew he would have to prove his valor in battle in order to gain a permanent place in Viking society.

Young Vikings had no formal schools to teach them the arts of war and survival at sea. Their schools were the oceans and rivers, and the battlefields. They learned to navigate and master storms at sea, and to fight for their lives against superior forces.

The Vikings not only conducted themselves like warriors, they looked the part. Though they did not wear uniforms as such, they dressed alike. Their trousers were of brown wool, strapped close to their legs with the thongs of their leather boots. Their tunic was long-sleeved and white and extended to their knees. Over it they often wore a shirt of mail, made of countless tiny interlocking rings of iron. And over all they would wear a sweeping cloak of red, orange, blue, or purple, with a cowl that could be raised against the rain.

Around their waists the Vikings wore belts of leather with buckles of gold and silver, and around their wrists and arms were bands of gold. Their headdress in battle was a round-topped or conical helmet of metal or heavy leather, sometimes with a protecting nosepiece. Helmets shaped as animal heads with wings or horns were rare and were apparently reserved for chiefs and nobles. The hair was worn long enough to cover the neck, and moustaches and trimly pointed beards were common.

They carried spears and bows and arrows, but these were often discarded after they used up the supply of arrows or hurled the spear at an enemy. Their principal weapons were the sword and axe. The axe blades were sometimes inlaid with bronze and silver decorations. The swords, which were carried in scabbards at the waist, were masterpieces of the weaponmaker's art. The double-edge blades were of tempered steel, and the hilts were beautifully ornamented with gold and silver inlays. Sometimes the blades carried runic inscriptions such as, "Let Siegfred's sword spare no one." Other symbols and inscriptions were evidently intended as charms against the enemy or invocations to the gods.

Their shields were circular disks of wood with a metal knob in the center which was cleated to the handle on the inner side. Wood seemed to be poor material for a piece of armor. But such a shield could deflect a spear or arrow and break the blow from a sword or axe.

While kings and chieftains had personal flags and standards, the flag that generally led the Vikings into battle had a special meaning to its followers. It depicted a raven in flight, pointed forward toward the flagstaff. The raven would "fly" only when the banner was moving steadily forward in the wind. If the troops hesitated, or shrank from battle, the raven drooped and fell—signaling misfortune to the Vikings.

A Viking might be quick to engage in personal combat if he knew he had been wronged. But usually Vikings did not fight with each other, apart from fencing and wrestling matches. They did not have to demonstrate their bravery with one another. Courage was something exhibited in combat with an enemy. Otherwise it was taken for granted in Viking society, where cowardice was unthinkable.

There was one special class of Viking warriors who were held in awe and were much feared by their enemies. These warriors were called *berserkers*.

The berserkers, meaning bare-shirts, were Vikings who fought with almost insane ferocity. In the midst of battle they tore off their shirts of mail and fought with their bare hands, ignoring any wounds that they received. Some of the sagas tell of a group of brothers who were mighty berserkers. When the urge to violence came upon them, they would wrestle with trees or giant boulders to keep from attacking one another. Today the term *berserk* is still used in English to mean loss of reason, or an impulse to sudden, extraordinary acts of violence.

In general, however, the Vikings fought with discipline and strict obedience to their leaders. Their overseas raids were not the wild acts of an uncontrolled mob. The raids were carefully planned and their success was due to timing, teamwork, and the Vikings' concern for one another.

At first the overseas raids were aimed solely at acquiring plunder, silver and gold being much preferred. The Vikings did not fight unless they had to. They would appear before a seaside town, their ships bristling with spears, and demand ransom or *danegeld* ("Dane's money") to leave the town in peace. The terrified population would often submit to this demand, and the Viking ships would sail away deep-laden with bags of silver.

Such a payment, however, rarely assured the town of lasting safety. When word got around that such a town was able and willing to pay an enemy to disappear, the enemy would reappear, again and yet again, to collect his danegeld of precious metals.

As Viking raids continued and expanded, the coastal cities of France, England, Ireland, and Spain strengthened their fortifications and trained their troops in adequate defense. If the Vikings saw that a town was too strongly

move along the river with their ships wherever possible. If their targets were not on the river but inland, they left their ships and mounted the horses they had gathered. One does not think of the Vikings as cavalry, and strictly speaking they were not, but they went on horseback to places their ships could not reach.

Hanson Baldwin, the well-known military writer, notes: "The Vikings . . . possessed the best military brains of their age. Some genius among them observed this [cavalry] business, and in 860 comes an ominous entry in the *Anglo-Saxon Chronicle:* 'A great heathen army came out of the land of the East Angles and there was the army a-horsed.' "

The Vikings, however, did not fight on horseback as did the French and English. They preferred to dismount and fight on foot. They had their own battle formations. They advanced in wedges, with the leader at the point of the wedge and his men fanning out behind him. As one man fell, his place was quickly taken by the man behind him so that the wedge was never broken.

As they approached the enemy lines, they discharged their arrows like long-range artillery. Then, as they drew closer, they hurled their spears. Finally they closed in with axe and sword, and engaged in hand-to-hand combat to the death. Few prisoners were taken, none among the Vikings. The Vikings abhorred slavery for themselves, and preferred death to capture.

According to Viking religion, death on the battlefield was not the end. If a warrior died honorably, he would be carried away on the flying horses of the Valkyries, the hand-maidens of Odin, to Valhalla. This was the Viking heaven for heroes. Here he would live forever, feasting and singing in the company of fellow warriors. This heaven was so greatly desired that a Viking dying of sickness would beg his relatives to stab him, so that Odin might think he had died in battle and receive him into Valhalla.

Belief in Valhalla led to special funeral rites for Vikings. A Viking chief who had been an honorable warrior would be buried in his ship, along with his weapons and personal goods, his horse, and sometimes even a faithful slave who was willing to die in return for accompanying his master to Valhalla. The ship was sometimes burned and the chief cremated. But often it was buried beneath a mound of earth and clay where it was preserved for centuries.

Because of this custom several Viking ships have been unearthed in modern times, a thousand years after they were built. Two are particularly famous: the Gokstad ship and the Oseburg ship, named for the places in Norway where they were found.

The Gokstad ship, built around A.D. 900 and excavated in 1880, evidently belonged to a local Viking chieftain whose remains were found in a specially constructed burial chamber surrounded by his personal belongings. The Oseburg ship, slightly smaller and perhaps a hundred years older, was found in 1903. It was believed to be the luxurious vessel of a Viking queen, whose body was discovered with that of her servant. Among its elegant appointments were many samples of Viking art and ornamentation, along with a beautifully carved cart and several sledges to aid the owner in her long voyage to the other world.

Both vessels, excellently preserved and repaired, are now in the Viking Ship Museum outside of Oslo, capital of Norway. They show exactly what a Viking ship was like, and how it was made and equipped. This is important, for the Vikings' ships, which were known as "steeds of the sea," were the secret of their widespread conquests.

3

~~~~~~~~~~~~~~~~~~~~~~~~~~~~~~~~~~~~

"Steeds of the Sea"

The story of the Vikings is not only a story about people but about ships. The whole amazing history of the Viking people is linked to the ships they built and to the extraordinary voyages that these ships made possible.

Even before the Viking period began, boats were essential to life in Scandinavia. They were needed for fishing, for trading, for traveling from one place to another. There were few highways, and the surrounding sea, the lakes and rivers, took the place of roads.

At first these boats were simply family affairs. They were somewhat like the fishing dories that one sees today, "clinker built"—that is, with the planks of the hull overlapping one another for extra strength. They were meant to be rowed only, generally with a single pair of oars.

It was between the years A.D. 700 and 800 that the Vikings began to use sails. Probably they learned of sails from trading vessels that arrived from the south, perhaps from the Mediterranean countries where sails had been used for centuries. With this new development, the golden age of the Viking ships began.

Boatbuilding ceased to be a family affair. It became a matter for skilled professionals, each with his own staff of artisans. This made the vessels costly. But every chieftain, every earl, and certainly every king had to have one or more ships for trade or conquest.

The Viking ships were not mass produced from one single pattern. There were no plans drawn in advance. A ship's plan was in the shipwright's head, and as it was built he would measure each piece by eye. But the principles, the method of construction, never varied. And though each ship differed according to its intended use, all had a similar form that was graceful and lovely.

They were long and low, and sharply pointed at both ends. Seen from the side, the ship's lines flowed in a slightly curving sweep from stern to bow, ending in high rising posts. The ends of the posts were often carved to represent a dragon's or a serpent's head or tail. These fierce carved heads were to frighten enemies and to ward off evil spirits. For this reason the ships were sometimes called "dragon ships" or "serpent ships."

Along the sides, beneath the gunwale, or upper edge of

the vessel's open hull, were holes for oars. There were no fixed seats for the rowers to sit on, but it is assumed that they sat on chests that carried their belongings.

Beneath the gunwale, too, ran a railing where the Viking shields were fastened. These could be hung in a row outside the ship. They were painted in alternating colors and overlapped one another. The shields served as ornaments when the ship was resting in port—like badges testifying to the owner's rank. As a rule they were removed when the ship was moving through the water.

Although beams ran across the ship from side to side, to hold the hull in shape, there was no fixed floor or deck. Sometimes planks were laid loosely on top of the cross beams to provide for walking and standing. The pointed bow and stern were often planked over to provide small cabins for passengers and goods.

The mast rose from a wooden socket in the center of the ship. This was so constructed that the mast could be slipped in or out of the socket as needed—lowered, for instance, to pass beneath a bridge. But the mast was generally left standing when the ship was rowed. The sail hung from a single spar that was raised to the top of the mast and held there by a rope of seal or walrus skin. The sail was a large, square piece of wool, often white with stripes of red cloth sewed into it for reinforcement.

The ship was steered by an oarlike rudder fixed to the right side of the vessel, close to the stern. This "steer board" led to the modern term *starboard*, meaning the right side of a ship as one looks forward. The tiller, or handle of the rudder, extended crosswise over the stern of the vessel. It was moved forward or backward to turn the rudder and direct the ship.

One unusual feature of Viking ships was that the planks or "strakes" of the hull were fastened to the frame, not by nails but by bindings of roots or animal hide. This meant that the hull of the ship was not stiff or rigid. Though watertight, it was pliant and elastic. It "gave" with the pounding of the sea, instead of breaking. And because of this the ship moved like a live thing through the water, twisting and squirming like a fish or serpent.

In fact, the Vikings thought of their ships as living creatures. They gave their vessels such names as *Crane*, *Bison*, *Reindeer*, and *The Long Serpent*. They thought of their ships, and spoke of them, with exultant pride, as suggested by these lines from the great Anglo-Saxon epic *Beowulf*, based on Norse legends:

> He gave command for a goodly vessel
> Fitted and furnished . . .
> Came the hour of boarding; the boat was riding
> The waves of the harbor under the hill.
> The eager mariners mounted the prow;
> Billows were breaking, sea against sand.
> In the ship's hold snugly they stowed their trappings,
> Gleaming armor and battle-gear;
> Launched the vessel, the well-braced bark,
> Seaward bound on a joyous journey.

Over breaking billows, with bellying sail
And foamy beak, like a flying bird
The ship sped on . . .

Because the hull of the ship was loose and lively, the keel, which ran along the bottom of the boat from stem to stern, had to be extremely strong. It was carved from a single piece of oak, and the size of the ship might often depend on the size of the oak tree available. Though the measurements varied from ship to ship the dimensions of the Gokstad ship, discovered in 1880 near the Oslo Fjord of Norway, are thought to be typical. These measurements are approximately:

Length, stem to stern, 76 feet.
Beam, width amidships, 6 feet, 4 inches.
Height, bottom of keel to gunwale, 6 feet, 6 inches.
Weight, 30 tons.
Draft, depth below waterline, 3 to 4 feet.

The Vikings themselves measured their ships in different terms. They spoke of length in terms of "rooms." A room was the space needed for one pair of rowers, generally about three feet and corresponding to the distance between cross beams. Thus the Gokstad ship, with 16 pairs of oars, would be spoken of as a 16-room ship.

What a Viking ship carried in the way of crew and equipment would depend on its mission. Thirty to 45 crew and passengers would have been average for the Gokstad ship. Because there was no large central cabin, almost all vessels carried a tent that could be stretched over two thirds of the open hull. In port, the tent could be moved to shore as a temporary home or shelter.

All Viking ships designed for piracy and raiding were called longboats. These were lengthy and narrow, with low sides. Speed was the important thing, and these slender vessels cut through the water like a knife. Because they were light they could be beached quickly, or carried around obstructions in a river.

At first, in the ninth century when their overseas marauding started, the Vikings did not engage in battles at sea if they could help it. It was not necessary. Most of the countries they raided did not have navies to defend themselves. The Vikings would swoop down on the unprotected coast and do what fighting was necessary on the land.

Later, however, from the tenth century on, their enemies and victims also began to build warships to intercept the Vikings at sea. So the Viking longboats were made larger—became, in fact, battleships. They had high sides to protect the archers and to prevent boarding by the enemy. These later, larger ships depended more on oars than on sails for the tricky maneuvering required in sea fighting.

One such battleship was *The Long Serpent*. It was built in the winter of 999–1000 for Olaf Tryggvason, one of the great Viking kings of Norway, and though its remains have not been found it is described in several of the sagas. *The Long Serpent* was 129 feet long, with 34 rooms for 34 pairs of oars. That was about as large as a Viking ship could safely be, since the keel was cut from a single piece of oak.

Most of the longboats were between 20 and 25 rooms in size. But when one reads of a raiding fleet of 200 ships one can assume that the fleet consisted of many different sizes—smaller ships for darting in and out of the enemy defenses and larger ships to serve as fortresses.

In later ventures the Vikings crossed the ocean to Iceland, Greenland, and America. But these lengthy voyages called for ships that differed somewhat from the longboats. They were broader and larger, with high sides to hold back the waves. These ships were called *knorrs*.

Knorrs were the work ships of the Vikings. They carried cargo on trading voyages, or passengers on expeditions overseas. When there were many passengers the ships also had to carry plenty of provisions. These would sometimes include live cattle and chickens as well as sacks of grain and fruit, dried fish and salted meat, and buckets of fresh water. Tools and lumber might be carried also, to build shelters and homes after the voyagers had landed.

The knorrs were designed primarily for sailing rather than rowing. The mast was often fixed solidly in the hull and rarely lowered. As standard equipment on overseas voyages these ships carried at least one small boat, lashed to the cross beams on deck. It was clinker-built like the parent ship, and fitted for two or three pairs of oars. This "after-boat," as it was sometimes called, was used for traversing from ship to shore when the parent vessel could not get close enough to land and for exploring shallow estuaries and rivers. Aboard the knorr, too, would be one or two wooden beds for the owner and his family, and sometimes a cart or a sledge for travel on land.

For 300 years the Viking ships were masters of the sea. It was only when the nearby countries of France and England, especially the latter, learned to copy the Viking vessels and built up great navies of their own, that the Viking ships lost world supremacy. And when the ships lost their supremacy, so did the Vikings. A Viking ship was as much a part of the Viking man as the horse was to the pioneer settlers of the early American west.

4

Building a Viking Ship

How would a Viking chief have a longboat built for his personal use? First, he would employ a professional shipwright. There was one in every large community. The shipwright had a staff of 10 to 12 workers, each one a specialist at his particular job. For example, there was one expert at cutting the planks, another skilled at fitting the joints, and yet another did the intricate carving of the bow and stern posts.

Shipbuilding was a winter occupation in the Northlands, for the summers were needed for tending the crops or for trading and raiding overseas. But the wood might be selected well ahead of time, and stored in a pond or watery bog to keep it fresh and supple.

The ship was eventually put together on a flat, convenient beach. But much of the shaping of the planks, and all of the decorative carving, was first done indoors—in the great hall of the house where there was ample room to work on planks and spars. The oars, too, might be shaped indoors.

As soon as the spring weather came the materials were taken to the beach and laid out, ready for assembling. A rough cradle or frame was erected to support the sides of the ship as it was being put together.

First came the keel because its size determined the over-all size of the boat. The keel piece was selected well ahead of time. This involved finding a tall, straight oak tree. A tree 80 feet high might make a keel 60 feet in length, after the narrow top was chopped off.

Using axes and gouges the Vikings shaped the trunk to a 12- or 14-inch-square log. The upper side of this log, on which the hull rested, was made slightly wider than the under side. This additional width was needed for nailing down the bottom strakes or planks.

When the keel was in place, the workmen attached the bow and stern posts. These were of the finest oak that could be found, for the posts formed the cutting edges of the vessel, splitting the water at the bow and resisting the water at the stern. The posts might be from 12 to 14 feet high, and the tops probably were carved to represent a dragon or a serpent.

The bow and stern posts were not attached directly to the keel. That would have made too sharp an angle. A

curved piece of oak was placed between them, leading from the ends of the keel to the bottoms of the posts. All three, keel, curve, and posts, were fastened together with strong iron nails. The joints were generally mortised, so that a curved projection on one piece fitted into a corresponding cavity on the other.

Next came the ribs. These, with the cross beams, formed the skeleton or internal frame of the ship. In the Gokstad ship, for example, there were 19 ribs. Each was cut from a single piece of oak that had grown naturally into the shape of a U, this U-shape corresponding exactly to the shape of the hull. Needless to say, the Vikings had to search extensively through the forests to find 19 rib pieces of this same unusual formation. Today one would steam or boil pieces of wood and bend them to the desired shape. But all curving parts of a Viking ship were cut from naturally curving wood for greater strength.

The ribs were squared off on all sides and on the ends. Then they were placed upright on the keel at three-foot intervals. The ribs were not fastened to the keel but simply rested there, later to be fastened to the planking. Across each rib from top to top were nailed the cross beams to keep the ribs steady and in position. From the top of the rib, where it joined the cross beam, rose the "knee." This was an upright piece of wood that extended from rib to gunwale and supported the topmost planks of the hull.

Next came the planking, or "skin," which formed the sides and bottom of the ship. For this the Viking shipwrights needed 32 planks, 16 per side, each one cut ideally from a single piece of oak. Because the Vikings had no saws, these planks were cut and trimmed entirely with axes and chisels. Yet all but four of them were made only an inch thick. The planks at the water line (tenth from the bottom) and the planks containing the oar holes (four-teenth from the bottom) were cut slightly thicker, one and a half inches, to provide for the extra stress at these points.

One might think that these planks were much too thin to withstand the buffeting of stormy oceans. But oak is both strong and elastic. The planks would bend but they would not snap from the pressure.

When, around the year 1000, King Olaf Tryggvason's

ship, *The Long Serpent,* was being built, the master ship-wright Torberg was absent when the planks were cut. According to the Norse historian Snorri Sturluson, Torberg's workmen sought to make the ship stronger by cutting the planks thicker. But when the ship was finished and Torberg returned to see the thicker planks, he took a chisel and gouged out a hole in every one, demanding that each plank be trimmed to the depth of the hole. Lightness and suppleness were twin secrets of the Viking ships.

The Vikings did not nail the planks to the ribs, which might seem the simplest method. Instead they tied them to the ribs with strands of animal hair or spruce root. To do this they had to carve, in the middle of each plank, 19

wooden cleats corresponding in position to the 19 ribs. This was a great deal of work, and it is easy to see that cutting, trimming, and carving the planks took a good part of the winter months.

The planks were next laid so they overlapped, the bottom edge of one lying over the top of the plank beneath it. The two planks were fastened together with nails, several inches apart, that passed through both and were riveted to small metal plates on the inside. Once both sides were fastened together, the seams between the planks were caulked with animal hair dipped in tar for waterproofing.

Now the side and bottom planks were lashed to the ribs from the inside of the ship. The 19 cleats carved in the center of each plank, on the inside surface, were at intervals corresponding to the three-foot intervals of the ribs. Holes were now drilled at corresponding points in each rib. The lashing of hide or root passed through these holes and around the cleats, then back through the holes to be knotted on the inside of the ship.

It was this method of lashing the planks to the ribs that gave the Viking ship its pliancy, allowing it to writhe and twist through the water without breaking. When a replica of the Gokstad ship was built and sailed across the Atlantic in 1893, the hull was found to bend as much as six inches from stem to stern, yet it never so much as leaked, much less broke at any point. Because of this built-in liveliness, the ship reached a speed of 10 knots, or about 11 miles

an hour, on the crossing. This is a good speed for a modern sailing yacht.

Around the top of both sides of the ship ran the gunwale, a four-inch-square beam of oak or spruce that served to reinforce the graceful, sweeping lines of the hull.

In the third plank from the top, 16 holes were bored on each side of the ship for the 16 pairs of oars. The holes were positioned midway between the ribs. A horizontal slit was cut on each side of the hole so that the oar blades could be slipped in or out from the inside of the ship. Wooden disks pivoting on a nail at the top of each hole served as shutters to keep out the water when the oars were not in use and the ship was under sail.

The oars were cut from pine, and varied in length from 17 to 19 feet. The shorter oars were used at the center of the ship. Toward the bow and stern longer oars were needed because the rising sides of the ship increased the distance from the water. The oar lengths were adjusted to this distance so that all the blades would strike the water at the same time.

Above the oar holes and parallel to them ran the shield rack, a railing where the handles of the Viking shields were tied when the ship was in port.

The mast was a single shaft of pine, about a foot thick, rising to 40 feet or more in height. It stood in a hole or socket in a block of oak about 12 feet long and a foot high. The block was fastened to the ribs in the center of the ship.

On the cross beams immediately above was the mast "partner," another block of oak with a hole that the mast also passed through. Thus the mast was supported at two levels. This upper block had an open slot toward the stern, so that the mast could be swung up or down without removing it from the socket in the lower block. When the mast was raised the stern opening was blocked with a wooden wedge.

Because sails were made of cloth, only fragments of them survive from the Viking era. From pieces that have been recovered, archeologists think that the sail was between 20 and 30 feet square, striped with red or dyed solid red or solid purple. The spar or yardarm to which the top of the sail was fastened slid up and down the mast by means of a wooden loop at its center. A halyard or rope attached to the loop would raise the sail, after which the halyard was tied to a cleat near the stern.

Because Viking ships had a single square sail, it had been thought that they could sail only before the wind. This is not so. There were cleats on the deck or cross beams to which the bottom corners of the sail could be stretched fore-and-aft, parallel to the keel. With the keel and the rudder blade, the ship could then sail crosswise to the wind and sometimes even *into* the wind.

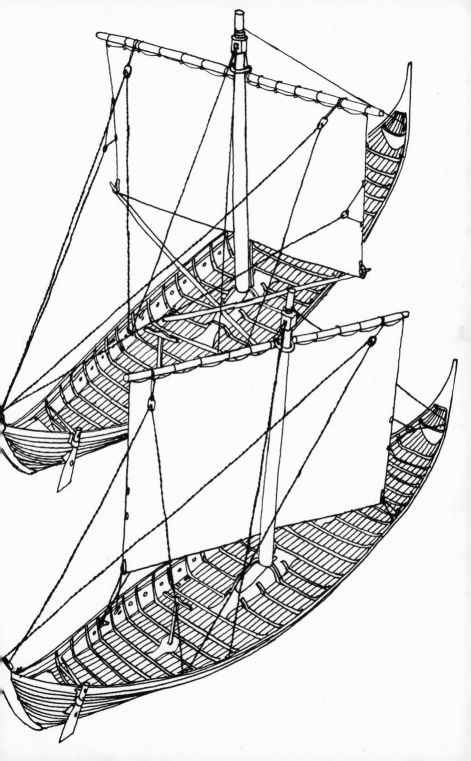

Finally there was the rudder. It was actually an over-sized oar about 10 feet long with a 16-inch-wide blade. It was attached to a knob of wood fixed to the outside of the ship. This was nailed to the planks and the sternmost rib above the waterline. Lashings of twigs or roots held the rudder to this block, loose enough for it to turn freely.

In normal position the blade of the rudder extended 18 inches below the keel, with its neck through a second loop of animal hide fixed to the gunwale. If this loop was released, the rudder could be pivoted upward when the ship was beached or was sailing in very shallow water. The handle or tiller was fixed to a hole in the neck of the rudder. It was about three feet long and extended across the stern of the ship at right angles to the rudder blade.

The completed ship might be painted red or black, favorite Viking colors, with gold paint for the carved decorations on the bow and stern posts. And the Vikings generally added a small boat to be carried on the cross beams.

They also added an iron anchor, shaped exactly like a modern anchor. It was kept in the bow with its line of walrus hide. It did not have to be large, for the Vikings never anchored their boats in deep or unprotected water. Generally they tied the bow to some solid object on land, and the anchor was used to keep the stern from swinging back and forth off shore.

Before setting sail the Vikings might also take a tent, to be raised over the hull when desired. It might be 18 feet long by 28 feet wide, and would hang over a ridgepole supported on two pairs of narrow boards nailed together near the center so that they opened like a pair of scissors. Boards running from bottom to bottom of these open struts kept the frame upright as it rested on planks across the center ribs.

This Viking ship was swift and sturdy, good for short ocean voyages and for cruising on sounds and rivers. It was very close to the famous longboat that the Vikings dearly loved, and with which they built their reputation as fierce sea adventurers.

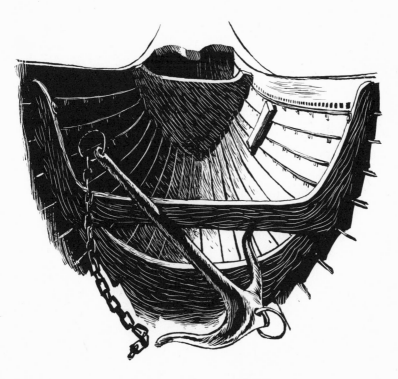

5

How They Navigated

Imagine a small band of Vikings setting out across the North Atlantic in an open boat with a single sail, bound hopefully for a land they have heard lies somewhere over the horizon. They have no maps or charts to follow, no compass to guide them, no modern instruments for fixing their position by the sun and stars.

How do they navigate, or sail their boat? How do they know what course to hold? After hours of sailing in high seas with a strong wind, how do they know if they are still on course?

Questions like these must have plagued the early Vikings, until they found the answers by experience and trial and error. In time they became expert navigators, crossing and recrossing the North Atlantic almost at will. Though there are records confirming that they were often blown off course, and landed in unexpected places—in fact, such un-intended landings sometimes resulted in major discoveries—they almost always found their way back safely.

One must remember that when, in the late ninth century, the Norsemen first set out on distant voyages of discovery and exploration, there was none among them who had previously ventured out into the broad Atlantic. There was no one to give them guidance and instruction. There were, however, other great seafaring people of that period, notably the Basques and Arabs. And it is possible that on some early trading voyages the Norsemen picked up certain sea lore from the Basque and Arab sailors. But for the most part they must have depended on their own experience and ingenuity.

They did have one advantage that the Basques, Arabs, and earlier sea adventurers did not have. The Viking ships were steady and dependable. The Vikings knew that if they settled on a course their ship could hold it. Except on rare occasions it would not be battered or blown off course by waves and wind, as were the unstable sailing ships of later mariners.

When it first came to navigation out of sight of land the Vikings learned to think in terms of latitude—that is, the distance south from the North Pole, or north and south from any visible object in the sky. They had no globes or maps in the modern sense, where latitude is shown by parallel lines running horizontally across the map.

The Vikings' greatest guide in determining latitude—in fact, their greatest aid to navigation—was the North Star, known to them as the Guiding Star. Simple observation taught them that it was a heavenly body that never moved, never changed position by month or season. Almost all the Vikings' long-distance sailing out of sight of land was done by estimating their position in relation to the North Star.

There was one difficulty in this dependence on the North Star. The Vikings did most of their overseas voyaging in the northern latitudes, where the summer nights are short and the North Star is visible for only a few hours. Accordingly, the Vikings planned their voyages for early spring or as late in the summer as possible, when longer nights made the North Star visible for longer periods.

To determine their latitude or position in relation to the Guiding Star, the Vikings developed a wooden instrument that the sagas refer to as a *husanatra*. The name probably meant a sighting device. It is not known exactly what this was like because none has been discovered among surviving Viking relics.

However, it is easy to imagine what a *husanatra* might have been. It may have consisted of a stick about three feet long, with notches carved in it at regular intervals. The stick would be held vertically on an even surface. With the eye kept at the same distance every time, the North Star would be sighted against the upright stick and a mental note would be taken of the notch that lined up with the star. If, in sailing along a desired latitude, the North Star crept above or below that notch, the navigator would know that he was off course. He would bring his ship back to a position where the North Star appeared at the same notch as it did originally.

Another equally simple device would have been a piece of flat wood cut in the shape of a quarter circle. Its curved edge would be notched or marked at closely set intervals, evenly spaced. With one straight edge of this pie-shaped device resting horizontally on an even surface, the eye could then sight the position of the North Star on the series of notches on the curving edge.

The Vikings did not have a compass. The compass had been invented many centuries before, probably by the Chinese, but had not yet reached the countries of the Norsemen. However, they did have a sort of compass card for checking directions.

This was a circular piece of wood or metal, the rim of which represented the horizon. The circle was divided into eight triangular segments called *airts*, corresponding somewhat to the eight principal directions shown on the modern compass. By placing the disk on a level surface, with the northern airt pointed to the North Star, the mariner could note the direction in which he was sailing.

This device was probably not used for finding direction but, rather, as a means of recording it for the benefit of others. In giving verbal directions to a fellow Norseman, for example, the mariner could refer to Iceland as being in the northwest airt if one started out from Denmark.

Navigating by the North Star the Vikings came on numerous landmarks such as rocks and islands. Eventually they found major islands such as the Shetlands and Faroes north of Scotland, and even Iceland and Greenland to the far west. In time they were then able to set their course in advance and sail according to such landmarks.

Because the handle of the rudder extended partly across the ship, and was pushed forward and backward rather than from side to side, the helmsman could face in either direction. He could face backward as the ship moved away from the point of departure, keeping this landmark in sight until it disappeared over the horizon. Then he would face forward, ready to pick up the next landmark as it became visible off the bow.

The effectiveness of this landmark navigation was increased by posting a lookout atop the mast. At a height of 50 feet a lookout could spot the top of a 7,000-foot mountain, for example, from a distance of 125 miles. As Viking historian Farley Mowat points out, this distance could be further increased by the mirages common to northern latitudes. Essentially the reflection of an object in the sky, due to atmospheric conditions, a mirage could increase the range of visibility by as much as 40 percent.

Between one visible landmark and another, however, there were long stretches in which the Viking mariner had no visible signposts to guide him. He might know his latitude, but he did not know how far he was from the landmark he had left behind and how far it was to the one toward which he was sailing.

He would have to rely on dead reckoning, a common

method still in use today. Dead reckoning means comput-
ing the speed of the ship, allowing for downwind drift,
and calculating the distance sailed in any given day or
unit of time.

To calculate the speed of the ship, the Vikings resorted
to the almost universal method of dropping a piece of
wood from the bow of the ship and noting the time it took
to reach the stern. This time interval could be measured
by a sand glass, possibly obtained from French or Mediterranean traders; or, in the case of romantically inclined
Vikings, by a poem that the mariner began to recite as the
wooden float was dropped.

An equally common method was to attach to a log of
wood a line made of animal hide or tree roots, with knots
tied in it at regular intervals. The log would be dropped
from the bow, and as it drifted past, count would be kept
of the number of knots that passed the stern in a given
unit of time. From this method comes the modern term
knot, meaning one nautical mile per hour, as a measure-
ment of a vessel's speed.

Speed and distance were also combined by the Vikings
in a unit known as a *doegre*, or day. At first the doegre was
based on the average distance a six-oared boat could be
rowed between sunup and sundown. Later, when the
Vikings took to sail, the doegre was redefined to mean the
average distance a ship could sail in 24 hours, or 120 miles
a day.

Thus, knowing his latitude and knowing how fast and

how far he was sailing, the Viking mariner had a good idea of both his course and his position at any time during a lengthy voyage between landmarks.

In addition to these crude devices and methods the Vikings had other navigational aids based on their extraordinary awareness of natural phenomena. They knew from the feel of the wind on their faces and the direction of the waves whether or not they were holding to a true course. If the wind changed direction they sensed it immediately and altered course accordingly.

The Viking mariner took other hints from nature. He knew that the sight of shore birds indicated that land was near. Certain fish known to be common at certain places in the ocean could help to tell him where he was, and the same was true of whales, which were known to frequent particular corners of the northern seas.

Sometimes a Viking ship would carry a few ravens aboard. Ravens are land birds, and when released at sea will quickly head for the nearest land. By releasing a raven and following the direction of its flight, the Viking helmsman could arrive at a landfall that he could not see.

When they first set out to explore the uncharted ocean the Vikings had no maps. But after many years of sailing by landmarks and arriving at distant shores they were able to draw crude charts for the benefit of fellow mariners. These were inscribed on hides or slabs of wood, and some survive today, transcribed on parchment around 1500. Such charts showed only rough outlines of the shores encountered and the approximate positions of islands and landmarks on the way.

Of far more use than such charts, however, were the word-of-mouth instructions passed down from one generation of mariners to the next, and appearing often in the Viking sagas. Farley Mowat condenses these instructions in a typical order:

1. The departure landmark.
2. The direction, in airts.
3. The distance out of sight of land.
4. The arrival landmark.

This short list makes the Viking method of navigation seem extremely simple. It was. But it worked—perhaps because of the Vikings' love and knowledge of the sea. To them the ocean was not a strange and hostile expanse, peopled with vicious monsters and traps for the unwary (as it was regarded by the early Mediterranean mariners). It was a glorious, friendly highway to adventure, and they took to it with confidence and optimism.

6

South Through France

The Viking lands of Scandinavia faced the open ocean in only one direction: west. To the south and the east lay the inland seas and rivers of Europe; and the Vikings—as they began their voyages for plunder shortly after A.D. 800—quickly learned to navigate these waterways to their treasure-laden targets.

France, in particular, is a country of rivers. Rivers penetrate the land from three directions: the Seine from the English Channel in the north, the Loire and Garonne from the Bay of Biscay on the west, and the Rhone from the Mediterranean in the south.

Inland the branches of these rivers spread like groping fingers, almost touching one another in the center of the country. Even today, despite hydroelectric dams on many of the rivers, one can go by water almost anywhere in France and return by a different route from each excursion.

These rivers made France an early target for the Vikings. For rivers were the highways of trade, and great cities rose along their banks. The cities supported monasteries and cathedrals, richly decorated with ivory carvings, jewels, and gold and silver ornaments—tempting bait to the Vikings from the north.

In the first half of the ninth century, when the northern pirates first broke loose from Scandinavia to go i-viking, France and much of the rest of Europe was a united empire under Charles the Great, or Charlemagne. The Franks who inhabited it were Germanic tribes who had usurped the land from its Roman conquerors. Though the Frankish empire gave its name to modern France, the Franks themselves were only one early element in what constitutes the French people of today.

Charles, a wise and knowing monarch, was well aware of the Viking threat. One incident had warned him. Early in his reign he had seen a Viking fleet approach his southern coast, intent on testing its defense. Though the marauders fled on learning of his presence, Charles reportedly wept at the sight of them, saying: "I do not fear that these worthless scamps will do any harm to me. No, I am sad at heart thinking that while I live they dare intrude upon this shore. And I am torn by a great sorrow foreseeing what evil they will do to my descendants."

As long as Charles the Great ruled France, the country

remained well defended. Strong walls were built around the cities, and the people were united against the foreign invader. Nevertheless, the king's apprehension proved correct. When Charles died in A.D. 814 he was succeeded by his son Louis the Pious, who ruled until A.D. 840. Thereafter the Frankish kingdom was partitioned among Louis' three sons, one of them, Charles the Bald, reigning over the western sector, which included much of present-day France.

With the kingdom split three ways among jealous and hostile brothers, France was greatly weakened. The military strategy of divide and conquer was half accomplished, to the benefit of the waiting Vikings. Down from the north they came, swarming up the rivers like schools of hungry sharks. In churches and cathedrals throughout the countryside the commonly recited prayer became: "From the fury of the Norsemen, Lord deliver us!"

These river Vikings differed from their ocean-faring brothers only in methods of navigation. In their longboats they were adept at maneuvering through narrow channels and twisting waterways, over natural and man-made obstacles such as shoals and dams. They knew how to make good use of the slow currents near the banks or the faster-moving waters in midstream. And they relied far more on oars than sails.

The Viking longboats themselves were admirably suited to the rivers. Because they were shallow, double-ended vessels they could reverse direction without having to turn around. The ships were so light in contrast to their size that they did not draw much water, and could easily be portaged around dams and bridges. And the clinker-built oak construction made the ships' hulls resistant to sharp rocks and floating driftwood.

The Vikings brought with them not only the tools of war—swords, axes, javelins—but work tools to trim trees for their fortifications and to build such devices as battering rams and catapults when needed to storm a city's walls. Generally the invaders would rely on obtaining food and horses from the surrounding countryside.

The rivers led to wealthy trading centers and cities rich with ecclesiastical treasures. These were, of course, the true goals of the Vikings. But they did not recklessly charge up the rivers to attack these settlements. There was a very definite method to a Viking invasion.

First they would establish a fortified base at or near the river's mouth. Thus the Vikings always had a haven to which they could retreat. While the main force raided upstream, a smaller force would remain at the base to protect the rear.

Most of the French river Vikings came from Denmark or southern Norway. So long as Charlemagne ruled his empire they limited their raids to nearby Frisia or what is now the Netherlands. But with the partition of Charlemagne's kingdom they felt free to invade France. They ringed the country with their river-mouth bases, and ranged far inland to the very center of the country.

The Norsemen became known by the rivers they occupied. Thus by the ninth century in France there were the Seine Vikings, the Loire Vikings, and Rhone Vikings. Often the Norsemen were in such complete possession of a river territory that they could successfully repel any other Vikings who attempted to intrude.

At the mouth of the Loire, for example, they first seized the island of Noirmoutier, on which stood a monastery. The monks fled at sight of them, and the monastery became a perfect fortress for the Vikings to fall back on after upstream raids, a place to attend their wounded and repair their ships.

From Noirmoutier the Vikings sailed up-river to attack

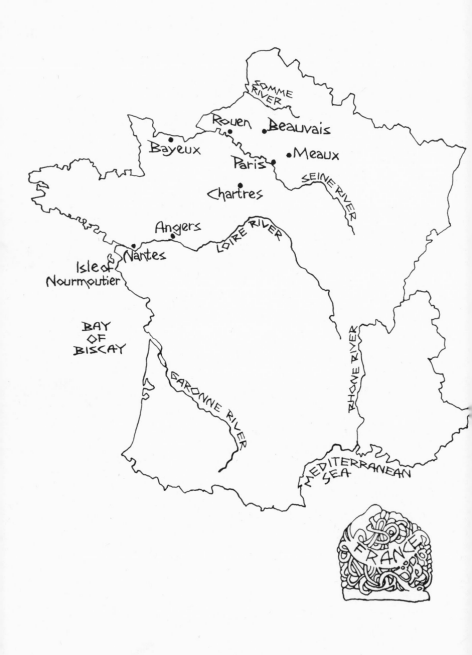

the rich cathedral town of Nantes. They arrived on St. John the Baptist's Day when the city was crowded with worshipers and pilgrims. Hidden by the river's banks the tall-prowed ships crept up to the city like a swarm of serpents. Once at the gates the Vikings stormed ashore with shield and sword to take the innocent city by surprise.

It was a murderous attack that illustrated the worst of the Vikings' ruthless methods. As one historian describes it, "They slew in the streets, they slew in the houses, they slew the bishop and congregation in the church. They did their will till nightfall, and the ships they rowed downriver were deep-laden with plunder and prisoners."

Some years later, not content with the sacking of Nantes, the Loire Vikings pushed farther up-river to capture the city of Angers on the tributary River Maine. Here they proposed to settle for an indefinite stay, making occasional raids up-river when called for, and bringing their families down from the north to farm the fertile river bottom land.

This effrontery shocked the Franks to action. To have a Viking outpost at the river mouth was one thing. To have a Viking-possessed city deep in the interior was quite another.

King Charles the Bald personally led an expeditionary force to drive them out. Angers was a walled city, and beneath its walls the Viking longboats were ranged like a ring of forts. Catapults and other machines of war were brought to bear against them, but the invaders held on.

Then Charles devised an ingenious scheme. He knew

how much the Vikings depended on the mobility of their ships. If one could not drive them from the river, why not take the river from the Vikings? Accordingly he engaged his army to dig a canal that would send the River Maine off in another direction and leave the Viking longboats high and dry.

A Viking with a grounded ship was like a warrior without a sword. The very psychological effect of seeing their vessels rendered useless prompted the Norsemen to surrender. King Charles' terms were surprisingly lenient. He agreed to let the Vikings return down-river unmolested provided they agree to leave the Loire for good. This the Norsemen readily agreed to, feeling free thereafter to raid other rivers in the Frankish kingdom.

7

The Siege of Paris

While the Loire Vikings were making life miserable for the towns and cities on that river, the greatest Viking river raids were raging on the Seine, the tortuous waterway that twists south into the heart of France. Paris, though not the capital of the Frankish kingdom, was the key city of that river valley. Beyond it lay the influx of the River Marne and the rich dukedom of Burgundy.

Leading the first assault on Paris was a Danish nobleman named Ragnar Lodbrok. Ragnar's second (or given) name, Lodbrok, was acquired, legend said, from his courtship of a Swedish princess named Thora. Thora's castle was surrounded by a ditch filled with deadly adders. To lay claim to his future bride, Ragnar was forced to wade across that forbidding moat. He protected himself from the poisonous

adders by clothing his legs in animal skins turned hair side out—hence the name Lodbrok, meaning "Hairy britches."

In the spring of 845, after establishing his base at the mouth of the Seine, Ragnar led a powerful fleet of 120 ships up the river toward Paris. King Charles the Bald heard of his coming, and led an army to intercept him. But Charles made the mistake of dividing his army into two separate forces, placing them on opposite sides of the river.

Again, it was not necessary for the Vikings to divide and conquer; Charles' army was already divided. The Norsemen fell upon the weaker of the two divisions, routing it and taking many prisoners. The captives, more than a hundred in number, they hanged in plain sight of the second

French detachment. The horrified Franks fled, and Ragnar's ships proceeded up the river, foraging and plundering as they went along.

On Easter Sunday they came within sight of Paris and the ships sped forward, their tall prows moving silently between the grassy banks. At the city's walls the Vikings leaped from their ships and stormed through the weakly guarded gates. Mercilessly wielding swords and axes, they slaughtered all defenders in their path, and plundered the city's monasteries of rich supplies of gold.

But as long as Ragnar remained in Paris the Vikings were more than 200 miles from the safety of the sea, not to mention the shelter of their base. Charles the Bald could well have taken advantage of the Vikings' perilous position, but perhaps he knew that simply forcing the Vikings to retreat would lead only to their return when opportunity was ripe. Accordingly he resorted to the cowardly expedient of a bribe. He offered Ragnar 7,000 pounds of silver to withdraw and leave Paris in peace. Needless to say, the offer was accepted, for Ragnar had already stripped the city of its treasures.

Ragnar's pledge to leave the Seine in peace was worthless. A Viking's promise was binding only when given to another Viking. Twice in the next 20 years Paris was again attacked, once by Bjorn Ironside, a son of Ragnar Lodbrok. A chronicler of those tumultuous times wrote:

> Ships past counting voyage up the Seine, and throughout the entire region evil grows strong. Rouen is laid waste, looted and burnt; Paris, Beauvais, Meaux are taken. Melun's stronghold is razed to the ground, Chartres occupied, Evreux and Bayeux looted, and every town invested.

Charles the Bald, seeking any means that would rid his land of Vikings, resorted to a new strategy. He was aware that Viking armies often fought against their fellow Vikings and even hired out to foreign kings as mercenaries. He approached a Somme River Viking named Weland and offered him 3,000 pounds of silver to drive the Seine Vikings from their river base at Oissel.

With a fleet of 200 ships Weland attacked the Seine Vikings at Oissel, mauled them severely, and forced them to pay him 6,000 pounds of gold and silver to remain free. Weland thus collected from both sides of the warring factions. Having partially fulfilled his pledge to Charles, Weland thereafter joined other Viking hordes harassing France on other rivers.

As a consequence of the repeated threats to Paris the city's defenses were greatly strengthened. From the central island of Paris two bridges were constructed, one of stone and one of wood. Each bridge was protected by a tower mounted by 20 archers. Any waterborne horde attempting to surround the city or press past it into Burgundy would be stopped short at the bridges, where a hail of arrows could be rained upon their heads.

Paris, however, remained the prize goal of the river Vikings. In A.D. 885 an immense fleet of 700 dragon ships manned by 40,000 Danish Vikings under a chief named Siegfred swept up the river to attack the city.

It was by far the greatest Viking force ever sent against a single target, up to that time. The Seine was so jammed with ships, ranged prow to prow, that one could walk across them from one bank to the other. Opposed to this mighty armada were only 200 Frankish men-at-arms led by a gallant abbot named Joscelin and a count named Odo.

Siegfred sought first to come to terms with the defenders. The Vikings would leave Paris unmolested if their ships were allowed to pass the bridges and row on to Burgundy. The offer was rejected and the next morning the Vikings launched a frontal attack upon the town with slings and arrows. The defenders responded by hurling boiling oil and burning pitch on the heads of the invaders.

It was a day of heavy losses for the Vikings, but in due course they attacked again. This time they had battering rams and rock-hurling catapults, hastily constructed on the river's banks. They also had wooden shelters mounted on wheels, in which groups of Vikings could approach the walls protected from the rain of boiling oil that poured down from the city's ramparts. Again they were driven off, leaving the river clogged with Viking bodies. This mightiest of Viking hordes appeared at last to have met its match.

For two weeks the Danes rested, buried their dead, tended their wounded, and regrouped their forces. Then they were ready for another try. They concentrated their attack upon the weaker of the two defending towers, filling the moat around it with slaughtered animals and the corpses of their own men to gain access to the tower's base. When this failed, they ignited three of their ships—with so many dead they no longer needed as many ships—and pushed the ships against the tower, where they burned out harmlessly. After three days of raging battle, Paris still stood and the Vikings were still outside its walls.

This siege of Paris might well have been one of the greatest Viking defeats in history. But water, always the Norsemen's greatest ally, came unexpectedly to their support. A sudden February thaw resulted in a flood that swept downstream and wrecked the northern wooden bridge,

allowing a portion of the Viking force to press hastily upstream and on to Burgundy.

Siegfred, however, stayed behind with many of his men
to continue the prolonged siege of the city. In desperation
Joscelin and Odo appealed to King Charles for aid. The king
arrived with a formidable army, but used it simply to come
to terms with the attackers. He would not only let the rest

of the Vikings proceed upstream and plunder the country-side at will, but he would also pay them 700 pounds of silver if, upon their return, they would go back where they came from.

The gallant Parisians were understandably shocked at the offer. They refused to abide by it and forced the Vikings to drag their ships up the banks and portage them around the bridges. When the Danes returned the following spring to collect the danegeld of 700 pounds of silver, they were driven off by Parisian arrows and forced to withdraw to their base at the mouth of the Seine. They appeared at last to have learned their lesson, for Paris was never besieged again.

Not so the lower valley of the Seine, where the riverside cities were repeatedly plundered and even the inland city of Chartres besieged by a Viking chief named Rollo. The name of Rollo ranks high in Viking history, for his appearance marked a new development in Franco-Viking relations. The Franks and Vikings had been at war so long that the French king sought a lasting compromise.

In a treaty signed in 911 Rollo was offered the dukedom of Normandy with the provision that he should swear allegiance to the French king and adopt the Christian faith. Rollo abided by the terms, and for the first time in Viking history the Norsemen took permanent possession of a part of France. This also started a gradual conversion to Christianity among those Vikings having contact with Christian countries.

As the years passed, the Vikings of Normandy became Vikings of France, adopting the French law and language and remaining loyal to the king. But while Normandy remained at peace, the Normans never lost their Viking instincts to take up arms for warfare overseas. It was a Norman of Viking descent, William the Conqueror, who defeated King Harold of England in 1066 in the last successful invasion of the British Isles.

8

Misadventure in the Inland Sea

While Vikings stormed up the rivers of France, leaving their marks of pillage and plunder on almost every major city, other adventurous Norsemen looked toward Spain, the Mediterranean, and Italy. These goals took them farther afield, farther from their native bases than any previous expeditions. It was risky to venture so far to the south. But risk was like a tonic to the hardy Viking spirit.

To reach the Mediterranean the Viking ships had to sail down the English Channel and around the coast of Spain, and the Vikings rarely sailed around a country without sampling what it had to offer in the way of plunder. The Moorish kingdom of Spain was fertile territory, ripe, they thought, for harvesting. They knew little or nothing about the Moors, the Arab conquerors of Spain. But what was there to know—beyond the fact that no other people could stand up to the Vikings?

Armed with this conceit, in A.D. 845 an armada of 150 dragon ships sailed south from the River Loire to Spain. The Vikings tested the Moorish defenses at Gijón and Lisbon and found them far from wanting. In fact, the Moors were as skilled in amphibious combat as the Vikings. The Norsemen were severely mauled at every point they landed. They suffered heavy losses of men, and what was far worse, almost half their ships were sunk or captured.

It was characteristic of the Vikings never to accept defeat. If they lost ships and men they simply carried on with what was left. Now pride forced them to extend themselves beyond the limits of discretion. Though reduced in force, they daringly entered the Guadalquivir River in Spain and rowed upstream to the fortress city of Seville.

At first the city, taken wholly by surprise, capitulated to the Norse invaders. But before the Vikings had had a chance to amass their loot and count their prisoners, the Moors were secretly rallied to counterattack. This time it was the Vikings who were taken by surprise. Wielding scimitars and spears the Arab warriors drove the Norsemen back aboard their ships, and then formed an ambush on both sides of the river to block their passage to the sea.

Attempting to escape the trap the Vikings were crushingly defeated. Thirty more dragon ships were sunk or captured, and scores of Vikings were taken prisoner and hauled back to public execution in Seville. When the city's gallows proved too few in number, Vikings were strung up in the palm trees. Those not hanged were beheaded, and the heads distributed as souvenirs among the Moorish victors and their allies.

It would seem that the Vikings should have learned to keep their distance from the shores of Spain. In fact the Spanish Emir sent an emissary north to Scandinavia, probably to Denmark, suggesting that Moors and Vikings live in peaceful coexistence.

But the Vikings still smarted from defeat. Sooner or later they would have to have revenge. Sooner or later, too, they would have to invade the Mediterranean, the cradle of western civilization, and try to make that inland sea their own.

This became the goal of one of the most famous of ninth-century Viking captains, Hastein of Denmark. Hastein led a fleet of 62 ships through the Bay of Biscay south to Spain, but he had no more success with the Spanish Moors than did his predecessors. He was driven from the Guadalquivir and forced on down to the Strait of Gibraltar. Here his Viking forces plundered the city of Algeciras, then sailed to North Africa to secure a cargo of slaves for sale in Viking-held lands in the north.

Hastein found the Mediterranean free of any opposing navies, for the Greek and Phoenician ships there were engaged in peaceful trade throughout that inland sea. The Vikings could sail where they liked, and plunder almost at will. They raided the Balearic Islands and probed the soft

underbelly of France. Following the custom of the river Vikings, they established a base on the island of Camargue in the Rhone delta. They then pushed inland into southern France, pillaging the countryside as far north as Valence, returning to pass the winter at their delta outpost.

As Viking historian Gwyn Jones recorded:

> It had been a wonderful summer of sunshine and blue water, of fabled coasts and storied islands. They had sailed by two great kingdoms, passed the Pillars of Hercules, and sojourned in classical Africa. They had a vast booty and many captives, their losses in men and ships had been light. They had shown the dragon-head and shield-wall in new havens, and were poised for fresh adventures.

The fresh adventures lay in Italy, a land so far untouched by Viking fury. Here Rome, the Eternal City, beckoned with its promise of rich Christian treasure. It seemed only fitting to Hastein that he, one of the greatest of Viking chieftains, should conquer the greatest city in the Christian world.

The Vikings had, of course, no maps of the Mediterranean to guide them. All they knew of Rome was that it was on a river on the western coast of Italy. Accordingly, when they came to the River Arno they decided that was it. Sacking the city of Pisa on the way, the dragon ships pushed up the Arno till they came to a city "so big, so white, so splendid, so marbled, that what else could it be but Rome?"

Hastein thought of a ruse to get inside the city. He first

sent an emissary to the city's gates with a disarming story. The Viking hordes, the messenger explained, were merely unfortunate men who had been expelled from their homelands. They had been driven by storms at sea to the mouth of the Arno, and had come up-river seeking help and provisions. Their leader was mortally ill. Would the kind citizens take pity and let them in to purchase food for their starving band?

When this tactic failed, the Vikings tried another— reminiscent of the famous trickery of the Trojan Horse. They reported that their gallant leader, Hastein, had died, and on his deathbed had requested a Christian burial. Surely the city would let his followers enter to dig a grave for him on Christian soil.

The request was granted. Bearing ahead of them a wooden coffin, a column of Viking mourners marched sedately through the portals of the city. They gathered at the burial ground, where an officiating bishop blessed the bier. Whereupon the "dead" Hastein rose from his coffin and ran the bishop through with his sword. Immediately the other Vikings cast off their mourning robes and ran amuck throughout the city, killing and plundering at will.

It should have been a glorious day for Hastein's Vikings. But to their surprise they learned that the city was not Rome at all, but a far lesser town called Luna. Furious at being cheated by their own mistake, they set the city aflame, slaughtered all the male citizens, and hauled the women to their boats as slaves. The Vikings then filled their longboats to the brim with plunder and rode the current down-river to the sea.

Woe betide any coastal city on their passage back through the Mediterranean. Like wasps in search of honey, the Vikings fell upon town after town along the coast of southern France. They sailed north around Spain and entered the Arga River to capture the city of Pamplona. Holding its prince for ransom, they collected an immense sum, and returned, after three years of absence, to their Loire River base at Noirmoutier.

They had been cheated of fame and glory as the conquerors of Rome, they had stubbed their toes against the stalwart armies of the Moors. But at least they returned with slaves and booty to make up for these embarrassments.

9

Westward to England

"It is nearly 350 years that we and our fathers have inhabited this most lovely land, and never before has such a terror appeared in Britain as we have now suffered from a pagan race, nor was it thought that such an inroad from the sea could be made."

So wrote an ancient historian when, in 793, a Viking fleet of longboats swooped down on Lindisfarne in northern England to plunder and burn the local monastery. This was to be no isolated incident. It signaled the start of nearly three hundred years of Viking raids on England, during which the Norsemen established their own nation on English soil, defied the successive challenges of five great English kings, and left their ineradicable mark on English history.

At first they were almost entirely Danish Vikings who sailed due west across the stormy North Sea. The Danes established bases on the Orkneys and the Hebrides and on the Isle of Man, until they had England surrounded from the sea. Their raids followed the classic Viking pattern—swift attack from longboats—on such English cities as Southampton, London, Rochester, and Canterbury.

England in the ninth century was ill prepared to counter such invasions. The country was divided into seven quarrelsome kingdoms, unable or unwilling to unite in the defense of all. The ravenous Vikings bit and tore at these kingdoms like a pack of wolves descending on a prey of scattered sheep. The helpless kings could only rejoice when their neighbors, not themselves, were the victims of the Viking hordes.

Despite frequent raids, however, the Vikings at first made no organized attempt to conquer England. That came with the great invasion of A.D. 866 when a vast armada of Viking longboats, their sails almost blanketing the sea, descended on the eastern coast. They picked the weakest kingdom in Britain, East Anglia, as their target and swarmed ashore without encountering a hostile spear or arrow.

They were led by two sons of Ragnar Lodbrok, Halfdan and Ivar the Boneless. The latter had gained his nickname from an accident of birth that, supposedly, had given him gristle instead of ordinary bones. Ostensibly the sons had come to avenge their father's death, for, when Ragnar left the Seine in France in 845 and invaded the English province of Northumbria, the Northumbrian king ordered him hurled to his death in a pit of poisonous snakes.

The real purpose of the invasion, however, was the conquest and settlement of England. To prepare for this the Vikings spent the winter in East Anglia, planning their strategy and scouring the countryside for horses. So far horsemen had been used only for scouting purposes. Now horses were acquired to increase the mobility of the Norsemen on land just as the longboats gave them mobility at sea.

When spring came the Vikings pushed up the valley of the River Ouse by horse and boat and captured York, which they fortified and made their capital. Next they stormed up the valley of the Trent to Nottingham, where they rested for the winter. The following spring they backtracked to East Anglia, made a clean sweep of the kingdom, and captured the English king Edmund.

It would have been wise if they had simply held King Edmund captive. But as so often happened, Viking blood lust obscured their better judgment. Edmund was executed, not humanely but by the cruelest methods the Vikings could devise. One account has him tied to a tree and used as a target for Viking archers. In any event, Edmund became a martyr in the eyes of his countrymen, and a martyr often has the effect of arousing an irresolute people to full wrath against their tormentors. As long as the Vikings remained in Britain, the memory of King Edmund's martyrdom helped to strengthen English resistance.

Flushed with victory, the Vikings now sought to conquer

the strongest of the English kingdoms, Wessex, which occupied most of southwest England. King Aethelred of Wessex with his brother Alfred met the invading hordes at Ashdown, and there for the first time the Vikings were routed. Their cavalry had not yet acquired the experience and skill of English cavalry. Most of the Vikings dismounted to fight on foot. This put them at a disadvantage with the mounted enemy, which could charge through their ranks, then swerve and attack them from the rear.

After this English victory King Aethelred died. He was succeeded by his twenty-two-year-old brother Alfred, who was to be known throughout English history as Alfred the Great. The Vikings had by no means given up their campaign against Wessex, and young Alfred fought nine pitched battles against them during his first year as king. He was sufficiently successful to force the Vikings to sue for peace, though some accounts report that Alfred paid them danegeld to withdraw and to give up their attacks on Wessex.

In any event, the Vikings retreated to the north and spent the next five years in conquering central England. This gave them a vast strip of land, running from the River Thames—the northern border of Wessex—almost up to Scotland. The conquered territory became known as the Danelaw, or country under Dane's Law. It was actually a Viking nation occupying half of England.

But the Vikings had to have all or nothing. They still coveted the remaining kingdom of Wessex, which would give them all of England. In 877 they moved south again under the leadership of a new chief named Guthrum. Believing he had settled with the Vikings once and for all, King Alfred was wholly unprepared for this new invasion. His forces fell before the Viking swords and axes, and he himself barely escaped with his life. He went into hiding in a marsh in Somerset.

From this period of despair in Alfred's life comes a familiar legend. The disguised king sought refuge in the hut of a peasant woman who agreed to let him remain if he would watch over her cakes on the hearth and see that they did not burn. When she returned from her chores to find that the cakes had been charred to cinders while Alfred brooded on his fate, the furious woman heaped abuses on her unrecognized king.

From the marshes of Somerset, Alfred and a tiny group of followers waged guerrilla warfare on the Vikings, gradually drawing recruits to their cause from all over the south of England. In time they were strong enough to move in force against the Vikings. They surrounded Guthrum and his men and starved them into submission. The Vikings sought terms for peace, offering hostages as tokens of sincerity. Guthrum himself agreed to be baptized, to embrace the Christian faith, and to pay tribute to the church.

Whether this was a sincere or empty gesture hardly mattered. It won the confidence of Alfred who agreed to the so-called Treaty of Chippenham. This bound both sides to a policy of peaceful coexistence. More than that, it established England's official recognition of the Danelaw as Viking property, creating a divided England.

Had the Vikings been content with the kingdom they had won, they would have been far wiser. But to settle down as peaceful citizens was not in the Viking nature. Once a goal was achieved they grew impatient for the next goal to be won. Accordingly, in violation of the Treaty of Chippenham, they used the Danelaw as a base for quick lightninglike raids on Wessex, plundering churches, monasteries, and abbeys, and then retreating to their homeland.

Alfred grew weary of these hornet stings and resolved to chastise the Danes. With a much strengthened army, he drove them back into the Danelaw and for good measure conquered the fortified town of London on the border between the Viking and English lands. The capture of London was of no strategic importance, but it greatly increased King Alfred's prestige among his subjects.

He took advantage of this increased prestige to further strengthen and enlarge his army. He solved the problem of recruiting troops by enforced enlistment. The peasants had always shunned serving in the army because it left no one at home to tend their farms and fields. Now, says the *Anglo-Saxon Chronicle*, ". . . the King divided his levies into two sections, so that there was always half at home and half on active service, with the exception of those men whose duty it was to man the fortresses."

This reform came just in time. In 892 the second invasion of England swept upon it from the Channel, this one from the Viking settlements in France—250 ships from Boulogne, 80 ships under the Seine Viking, Hastein.

Alfred's army, however, was sufficiently reinforced to be able to contain the enemy and even force them back into the Danelaw. North of London, Alfred cornered a Viking fleet on the Thames and resorted to the device of digging trenches to divert the river, leaving the Viking longboats high and dry—the same tactic that had been used by the French at Angers under King Charles the Bald.

While Alfred had generally contained the Viking force on land, he now decided to create a navy that could intercept the Viking ships at sea, to check an invading force before it landed. But when it came to building ships the Vikings had no equal. Alfred built his vessels principally for size, twice as long as the Viking ships, with 60 pairs of oars. Not only were these ships unwieldy, but their inexperienced peasant crews could not handle them. They went aground, or broke apart, and generally caused the great king nothing but embarrassment.

In the year 899 King Alfred died, to be remembered as "the most effective opponent the Vikings had met anywhere in Europe since the death of Charlemagne in 810." He was succeeded by his son, Prince Edward. Edward, supported by his sister Aethelfleda, vowed to reconquer the Danelaw. Aethelfleda was a remarkable woman, a combination of Joan of Arc and a Viking-famed Valkyrie. She joined Edward in leading the English troops into the Danelaw where Aethelfleda personally brought the men to the very gates of York. When she died she was able to leave Edward king of all England south of the River Humber.

The Vikings made only one other attempt during this period to challenge English supremacy over Britain. This came not from the Danelaw, which by now had thoroughly submitted to King Edward, but from Norway and the Norwegian Vikings who had settled in Scotland and in Ireland.

The Norwegians who came from their own country and

from Ireland undertook to seize the throne of York. Their arrival was as distressing to the Danes as it was to the English under Edward. At about the same time, Edward died, to be succeeded by "that magnificent young prince" Aethelstan.

At about the same time, too, the Vikings who had earlier occupied Scotland, and who had hitherto played little part in the invasion of England, now rose under their King Constantine. They allied with the Irish Vikings and the Norwegians in a move to conquer northern England. The two sides, in the sporting manner of two teams arranging for a championship game, agreed to meet at Brunanburh on Solway Firth to fight it out.

Each side allowed the other time to prepare. When the opposing troops were fully mustered and their forces balanced against one another, the trumpets of both sides sounded, and the battle was engaged. It resulted in a complete victory for the English, with bloody losses on both sides. The surviving Irish Vikings fled to their ships and the safety of Dublin. Constantine's men fled north to Scotland. An unknown poet recorded that the English

. . . sought their own country, exulting in war. They left behind them, to joy in the carrion, the black and horn-beaked raven with his dusky plumage, and the dun-feathered eagle with his white-tipped tail, greedy hawk of battle, to take toll of the corpses, and the wolf, grey beast of the forest. Never until now in this island, as books and scholars of old inform us, was there greater slaughter of an army with the sword's edge.

The battle marked the end of one period in the Vikings' attempt to conquer England. They had been thoroughly checked, although only for a time. Aethelstan and the succeeding kings of England, Edmund and Eadred, the latter reigning to 955, were charitable toward the Danish Vikings remaining in their kingdom. Diplomatic relations were established with Denmark, and there was an exchange of ambassadors on both sides, some Danish Vikings coming voluntarily to serve under the English kings.

Indeed the five successive kings of England, from King Alfred on, were as much the heroes of Viking history in England as the Vikings themselves. But they had failed in one thing. For all their victories they had failed to create a united nation. The Danelaw remained a separate entity under the government of Viking jarls. And after Eadred's death there was no strong king to unify the country. England, after 150 years of warring with the Vikings, was once again open to Viking invasion from overseas. In time it would come.

10

The Invasion of Ireland

When the Vikings first set out from their homelands to plunder overseas, Ireland was well into its Golden Age, an age of religious fervor and medieval learning. It was a country of cathedrals, abbeys, and monasteries, each filled with gold and silver treasures and gem-encrusted relics of the church.

This and the fact that Ireland was only a two-days' sail from Norway made it a tempting target for the piratical Vikings. And Ireland was ill-equipped to defend itself. Though supposedly ruled by a high king at Tara, it was in reality divided into seven separate kingdoms under seven lesser kings, all hostile and jealous of one another.

These Irish rulers were completely unprepared when, in 819, the Norwegian Vikings started probing their coastline, plundering the monastery of Lambey near Dublin, and establishing island bases off their shores for future operations. Some of these bases were as far away as the Orkney Islands and the Isle of Man, but still within handy striking distance of the swift Norse dragon ships.

And the Norsemen made good use of their ships. Hardly a day passed that the seas were not studded with the red and purple sails of Viking longboats sweeping toward the Irish coast. The *Annals of Ulster* for 820 recorded that "the sea spewed forth floods of foreigners over Erin, so that no haven, no landing-place, no fort, no castle might be found, but it was submerged by waves of Vikings and pirates."

The invasion reached mass proportions with the appearance of a Norwegian prince named Turgeis. He is reported as leading "great sea-cast floods of foreigners into Eire, so that there was not a point thereof without a fleet."

Turgeis came not only to plunder but to conquer and rule. He established forts at places that later became important Irish cities: Dublin, Wexford, Waterford, Cork, and Limerick. He conquered the sacred city of Armagh, the ecclesiastical center of the country, and made it his capital as "king of all the foreigners in Erin." In the same arrogant vein he sailed up the Shannon River to take over the monastery of Clonmacnoise and there installed his wife as a pagan priestess, practicing heathen rites.

These irreverent offenses were too much for the pious Irish, who conspired to kill the interloper. According to

legend, a beautiful Irish princess lured him to a woodland tryst. When Turgeis appeared, the princess' "handmaidens" threw off their flowing gowns to reveal a band of sturdy Irish henchmen. They dragged Turgeis to the nearest lake and drowned him.

But Turgeis' death did not bring tranquillity to Ireland. News of his exploits had reached Denmark, where the Danish Vikings became jealous of the successes won by their Norwegian brothers. They arrived in fleets, 150 ships strong, to contest the occupation of the stricken country. Ireland now became a battleground of Viking against Viking, the "black Vikings" of Denmark (so called for their generally darker hair) pitted against the "white Vikings," the usually light-haired Norse from Norway.

There appeared on this confused scene a new element in the Viking history of foreign conquest. This was a sort of inner group composed of discontented Irish. They were known as the Gall-Gaedhil, or "foreign Irish." They were not, of course, foreigners but merely freebooters anxious to side with the winning team—"low-born adventurers whose swords were for hire." In time the Gall-Gaedhil women intermarried with the invaders, forming a core of true Viking-Irish.

The chaos of inter-Viking warfare was ended with the arrival in 853 of King Olaf of Norway, a kinsman of Turgeis. "With a great fleet he came, and so great was his strength that Danes and Norsemen alike submitted to him." Olaf united the quarreling Vikings, and organized them for

raids deep into the heart of Ireland, to previously unmolested targets far from shore.

This represented something new in Viking operations.
Hitherto their raids had been swift attacks from sea or
river, in which they went ashore long enough only to storm
a monastery or capture a stronghold, quickly returning to
the safety of their boats. Now, farther inland, the Vikings
were often obliged to fight as infantry, on foot, with an
eye to military tactics and formations.

They were not without a knowledge of such tactics.
Chess was their favorite game, and they knew the importance of planned strategy. One Viking ruse was to feign
retreat, withdraw, and lead the enemy to follow them.
When the Irish forces approached the center of their out-
stretched line, the Vikings on either flank would suddenly
press forward, coming together like the ends of an en-
circling net.

In one battle the Vikings are described as forming "a
solid, skillful, and firm rampart of strong coats of mail like
a thick, dark stronghold of black iron, with a green polished
wall of battle shields around their chiefs." The Irish had
no such armament, "had nothing to protect their bodies and
necks and gentle heads save only elegant tunics."

It is curious that the Vikings, in spite of their great num-
bers and experience in battle, never really conquered Ireland.
Something in the Irish spirit refused to surrender. Though
for the next hundred years seaborne Viking armies followed
one another in assaults on Ireland's shores, venturing deep

into the interior, there remained strong, isolated pockets of resistance.

Assorted Irish kings still held on desperately to their separate kingdoms, and they often sought to save themselves by siding with the Vikings in attacks against their neighbors. Or they cooperated with the enemy in any way they thought would keep their lands intact. They did not altogether yield, but they submitted to Viking aggression because they did not make a strong and united resistance.

Throughout most of the tenth century Ireland was plundered by successive waves of Vikings, who made the city of Dublin their unofficial capital. Its large protected harbor could shelter whole fleets of Viking longboats. It became a center of Viking trade and a port of entry for Viking reinforcements. As long as Dublin was in Viking hands, the Norsemen had a strong grip on the country.

Toward the end of that century, however, there appeared a figure destined to change the fate of Ireland and the course of Viking aggression: Brian Boru, celebrated in song and legend as one of the greatest heroes of Irish history.

Brian was born in 941, son of a minor king of southern Ireland. As a young boy he had witnessed the ruthless Viking plunder of his native land, and he vowed that he would some day even the score, if not rid Ireland altogether of the Viking scourge. Still in his teens, hiding in woods and caves, Brian and his brother led frequent guerrilla raids against Limerick, the Viking stronghold in the south. Their pitiful forces suffered many losses, and in time Brian's following was reduced to only 15 men.

Had he given up then, the fate of Ireland would have rested with the Viking hordes. But Brian vowed to continue the fight, and his persistence and dedication won him many recruits. In time he had a sufficient army to attack Limerick in force. He conquered the city and sent its ruling chieftain, Ivar, a descendant of Ivar the Boneless, scurrying north to safety. When Ivar returned the following year with reinforcements, Brian attacked again and this time killed the Viking leader.

His fortunes now were rising. When the king of Munster died, Brian seized that throne and gained new recruits from this southernmost Irish province. With an expanded army he attacked the neighboring province of Leinster, heavily populated with Gall-Gaedhil or Viking Irish, and subdued it, to become king of southern Ireland.

He now set his sights on Dublin, seat and symbol of Viking power, and in 999 laid siege to the city. The violent and bloody battle that followed led to the wholesale slaughter of the Vikings' Dublin army. But Brian charitably did not press his advantage. He allowed the Vikings to remain in Dublin while he pushed on to conquer the northern provinces, gaining for himself the title of Emperor of Ireland.

During the ten years of his uninterrupted reign, Brian was a wise and just ruler over Ireland. Even so, his Gall-Gaedhil subjects in Leinster smarted under their subjection.

They conspired with the remaining Dublin Vikings to revolt and established a rival kingdom based at Dublin. At first Brian closed his eyes to this development. Then, in 1013, he decided that Dublin must be conquered once and for all. He led his men against the city, but was repelled at the gates. It was then winter and Brian decided to wait until spring for the final encounter.

Both sides feverishly prepared for the great battle that they knew was coming. Brian scoured the countryside for recruits, until he had amassed the first truly national Irish army, 20,000 men, consisting of 70 separate divisions under as many separate flags. Sigtryg, chief of the Dublin Vikings, likewise sought reinforcements from overseas. Promising each the throne of Dublin in return for their support, he enlisted the aid of Sigurd of the Orkney Islands and Brodir of the Isle of Man, each commanding a substantial fleet.

By Good Friday of 1014 both sides were poised for battle at Clontarf on the shores of Dublin Bay. For the battle that followed, the name of Clontarf was to rival in history the names of Hastings, Waterloo, and Gettysburg. The Vikings' line was dangerously thin, two miles long, to protect their ships in Dublin Bay. That was its weakness. On one flank were the island troops of Sigurd and Brodir. In the center were the Leinster rebels, and on the other flank the Dublin Vikings.

Brian's troops were commanded by his son Murchard and his grandson Tordelbach. Tordelbach was only fifteen years old but, like Brian in his youth, already a seasoned fighter. While the battle was in progress, Brian, now over eighty, repaired to nearby Tomar's Wood where he spread an animal skin on the ground and knelt to pray for victory.

As dawn broke, the Viking pipes sounded their rallying cry, and a group of Leinster rebels charged from the center of the Viking line and fell upon Brian's troops with sword and axe. But the Irish borrowed a trick from the Vikings. They fell back before the charge until the Leinstermen were well extended, then closed in on them from both sides. Seeing their allies trapped, Sigurd's and Brodir's men moved forward to their rescue. Brodir broke through the Irish lines and came upon Brian in Tomar's Wood, slaying him with a stroke of his axe and shouting, "Now let man tell that Brodir felled Brian!"

However, from the start the Vikings were at a disadvantage. They fought with their backs to the sea, with no room for maneuvering beyond retreat. The Irish, on the other hand, were well entrenched on higher ground. Now they moved forward from those entrenchments, slowly pressing the Viking forces back against the shore. Axe clashed against shield and spear against mail as the hand-to-hand fighting left scores of dead and dying on the beach.

Soon the slow Viking retreat turned into a rout. Before they could reach their ships some 7,000 Norsemen, almost half of the entire army, were dead, along with the island chieftains Sigurd and Brodir. The Irish losses had also been severe, with 4,000 killed. Brian's son Murchard had fallen. Of Tordelbach it was recorded: "The king's grandchild,

but then of the age of fifteen years, was found drowned near the fishing weir of Clontarf with both hands fast bound in the hair of a Dane's head, whom he pursued to the sea at the time of the flight of the Danes."

It was a costly victory, but certainly one of the most outstanding examples of an indignant people resisting Viking invaders. Never again would the Norsemen threaten to rule Ireland, or feel free to roam the countryside for plunder.

But Brian's death was a major tragedy for Ireland. With no powerful king on the Irish throne, the country divided again into small and quarreling kingdoms. As for the remaining Irish Vikings, they accepted the bloody decision at Clontarf. Thereafter, for the most part, they engaged in peaceful trade, established themselves as Irish citizens, took wives from among their conquerors, and became part of the Irish culture that exists today.

11

Founders of Russia

Remarkable as it may seem, Russia was named and founded by the Vikings. Of course, the Vikings' Russia was not the Russia of today. It was a kingdom of city-states, ruled by Viking princes, extending the length and breadth of the Dnieper River valley and eventually reaching eastward to the Volga River. Most of this territory had been inhabited by Slavs, whom the Vikings first took over by peaceful invasion and then merged with—creating a nation of shrewd, hardy people, adept alike at war and trade.

The Vikings who founded Russia were almost exclusively Swedes, whose homeland faced east toward Russia and bordered on the Baltic Sea. They were as much concerned with trade as with conquest. In fact, they resorted to force only if they could not get what they wanted by bargaining and paying for it.

To the east the Baltic Sea bends into the Gulf of Finland, at the head of which lies Lake Ladoga. From Lake Ladoga the Vikings had two river routes to choose from: the Volkhov and Lovat rivers both leading to the Dnieper River and down to the Black Sea, or further east the Volga River leading south to the Caspian Sea. It was the Dnieper River valley that attracted the adventurous Vikings who established Russia. Those who chose to follow the Volga were mostly merchant Vikings who ventured as far overland as Baghdad, Persia, for the precious metals, silks, and spices they could buy with slaves and furs.

The first Viking chieftain to sail with his men through the Baltic Sea and into the territory of the Slavs was a Swedish nobleman named Rurik. Curiously enough Rurik's

forces did not arrive as hostile invaders. They came by invitation from the Slavs themselves. For the Slavic tribes had been rent by internal warfare, and they wanted peace. According to the *Ancient Chronicle,* a Russian history of those times, they sent word to the Vikings, saying: "Our land is great and rich, but there is no order in it. Come to rule and reign over us."

Needless to say, Rurik was glad to oblige. He took over the trading city of Novgorod on the Volkhov River and made it his capital. The land about it he partitioned among his lieutenants. His reign was typically Viking in character. What he wanted most from his subjects was not loyalty but loot—not only for his own use, but for trade with the city of Constantinople and countries to the south. He exacted tribute from every Slav community he governed. But though Rurik may have been something of a tyrant, he maintained peace.

Rurik's Vikings were known in the east as *Varangians*, meaning men who were pledged to one another. They were also known as *Rus*, the term from which the name Russia comes. *Rus* might be translated as red or ruddy, referring to the Vikings' blond hair and complexion. It is also possible that the name of Russia derives from the Scandinavian word *ruotsi*, meaning river people or rowing people, again referring to the Vikings.

The Varangians eventually extended their territory as far south as the city of Kiev on the banks of the Dnieper. The Dnieper flows into the Black Sea, and across that sea lay the richest, most glittering city in all of Christendom. This was Constantinople, known today as Istanbul. Then it was the capital of the Eastern Roman, or Byzantine, Empire. From the moment the Vikings first looked eastward, this Queen of Cities was an irresistible magnet to their greed.

Two of Rurik's lieutenants, Askold and Dir, obtained their chief's permission to raid Constantinople. It was a bold and reckless undertaking. They must have known the city was stoutly defended and would not yield easily, for at Kiev they assembled a mighty armada of 200 ships and 8,000 men. The ships built for this and later assaults on Constantinople were somewhat smaller than the Viking longboats, although of the same construction and design.

On the lower stretches of the Dnieper was a series of seven cataracts that presented the Vikings with their first hazard. When was the best time to navigate these rapids? When the river was low and the rocks quite visible? Or when the river was high with spring floods and the rocks submerged? The Vikings chose the latter, although they knew that the swollen water would turn each cataract into a raging torrent.

It is a tribute to the Vikings' skill that they shot these rapids without the loss of a single ship. However, when a cataract appeared obviously too dangerous to attempt, they hauled the boats ashore and portaged them around the riskiest stretches.

They arrived at the gates of Constantinople at a favorable time. The Byzantine emperor had taken his fleet into the Mediterranean to fight the Saracens, Arabian sea rovers who were threatening the city from the south. For a while it seemed to the Vikings that they could enter Constantinople unopposed.

But, the story goes, a miracle intervened. The bishop of the city took the cloak of the Virgin Mary from its sacred hiding place in the cathedral, dipped it in the waters of the Bosporus strait, and thereby invoked a great storm. The Viking ships were scattered far and wide and many were wrecked before they could reach safety.

Askold and Dir returned to Kiev. Following Rurik's death in 879, they were murdered by Rurik's successor, a Viking chief named Oleg, who was jealous of their power and wanted all of Russia for himself. Oleg established a kingdom of provinces, each province ruled by one of his princes. Thus Oleg might be called the founder of the Russian state, although he should rightfully share this role in history with Rurik.

"Oleg set himself up as a prince in Kiev," relates the *Ancient Chronicle*, "and declared that it should be the mother of Russian cities. The Varangians, Slavs, and others who accompanied him were called Russes. Oleg began to build stockaded towns and imposed tribute on the Slavs. . . ."

It was inevitable that Oleg, too, should set his sights on Constantinople. Having learned of Askold's and Dir's defeat—which he thought was partly due to weakness—he took no chances. He marshaled a tremendous armada of 2,000 ships and 80,000 men, ten times as large as Askold's forces, and roared down the Dnieper cataracts to the Black Sea and across to Constantinople.

He found the sea approach to the city blocked by a heavy iron chain that stretched from shore to shore. To get around this he beached his ships, built wheels to put under them, and turned them into land-roving fortresses that could be pulled or pushed into position. Over the protecting sides of each vehicle rose the helmets and spears of 40 Vikings. The ships were rolled to the gates of the city where the Vikings demanded its surrender.

The Byzantine emperor sought a compromise. It was plain that the Vikings were after silver and gold, silks and precious gems. In exchange the Vikings had furs, wax, honey, and slaves. Why not make a deal, engage in trade instead of war? The Vikings would be allowed to enter the city in small groups, goods would be exchanged in barter, and the Norsemen could return home peacefully with what they had come for.

The offer was accepted, and for a time trade flourished between Constantinople and Oleg's Vikings. But this happy situation did not last for long. Oleg was succeeded by a king named Igor, who wanted more immediate wealth than peaceful trade could offer. He decided to scrap the agreement and take Constantinople, with its rich supply of Roman treasures, by force of arms.

With a massive flotilla of 10,000 ships Igor appeared beneath the walls of Constantinople. Once again the emperor was off with his fleet in pursuit of the Saracens. Igor felt certain of an easy conquest. But the Vikings had not yet challenged the fighting prowess and ingenuity of the Byzantine defenders. Now they did—to their dismay.

The Byzantine naval forces had a weapon known as Greek Fire, which was much like the modern flame thrower. It consisted of highly flammable substances such as sulphur, quicklime, and naphtha, forced into a bronze-lined wooden tube and then ejected by a plunger. A Byzantine admiral had gathered the few ships remaining in the harbor and fitted them with this flame-spitting device. The ships now charged down upon the Vikings, spouting liquid fire like a host of dragons.

The Vikings fled in terror before this extraordinary

weapon. Many were burned to ashes, and their ships left aflame on the water. Those that survived sailed back into the Black Sea to regroup their forces. Then, vowing that they would not return home empty-handed, the Vikings started to pillage the unprotected countryside. The *Ancient Chronicle* records:

> Many sacred churches they gave to the flames, while they burned many monasteries and villages and took no little booty on both sides of the sea. Of the people they captured, some they butchered, some they set up as targets and shot at, some they seized upon, and after tying their hands behind their backs, they drove nails through their heads.

This terrorism was not to go unavenged. When the Vikings were finally ready to return to Kiev, and headed

for the mouth of the Dnieper, they were intercepted by the main Byzantine fleet back from battling the Saracens. Again they faced the terrible Greek Fire, and again their ships were burned, the Vikings leaping overboard to escape the flames. Below the floating bonfires of their ships, the Vikings drowned by hundreds.

With only a handful of his Viking warriors remaining, Igor managed finally to return to Kiev. Thereafter his dealings with Constantinople were in terms of trade instead of war.

Following Igor's death and a brief period of rule by his widow Olga, their son succeeded them as monarch of all the Russes. His name was Svyatoslav, and there is a description of him from a writer of that period named Leo Diaconus:

He was of medium height—neither too tall, nor too short. He had bushy brows, blue eyes, and was snub-nosed; he shaved his beard but wore a long and bushy mustache. His head was shaven except for a lock of hair on one side as a sign of the nobility of his clan. His neck was thick, his shoulders broad, and his whole stature pretty fine. He seemed gloomy and savage. On one of his ears hung a golden ear-ring adorned with two pearls and a ruby set between them. His white garments were not distinguishable from those of his men except for cleanness.

From this description, one sees that Svyatoslav was, in appearance at least, more Slavic than Scandinavian. This was a common development. The Vikings gradually acquired the physical characteristics and customs of the country they had conquered.

Svyatoslav, however, was a typical Viking in his love of warfare and aggression. He and his fellow Varangians deserted the rivers and took to horseback to extend their conquests to the inland territories. They united with the Byzantine forces to make war on the Bulgars to the west. From this encounter they emerged triumphant and helped rid Constantinople of one of its most dreaded enemies.

One other Viking or Varangian deserves to be mentioned. He is Svyatoslav's son, Vladimir. Though Vladimir continued to expand the Russo-Varangian empire with successful wars upon the Poles and Bulgars, his chief claim to fame rests upon his conversion, and the conversion of his people, to the Christianity of the Greek Church.

By demanding that his subjects embrace the Christian faith, and by spending much of his wealth and energy in building churches, Vladimir wrote a concluding chapter that is common to Viking history. Almost invariably their conquest of Christian countries led to their acceptance of the Christian faith and to their final assimilation by the peoples they had conquered.

12

They Were Merchants and
Seaborne Traders, Too

One thinks of the Vikings as pirates and plunderers, which indeed they were. But they were also great merchants and traders. Although the Vikings' land conquests and raids stand out in history, their extensive commerce with other peoples helped to establish the trade routes of Europe, western Asia, and the Middle East. Many modern European and Asian cities were originally Viking trading posts.

Two factors gave rise to this seaborne trade. First, Scandinavia had a strategic position on major water routes and the Norse were adept at shipbuilding and navigation. Second, Viking lands had many goods that other countries wanted. Among such goods were furs, hides, sea ivory from walrus tusks, antlers, soapstone, and birds' feathers for pillows.

Many of these arctic luxuries came from the Lapps, a people who still live and tend reindeer flocks in northern Scandinavia. Lapp goods were obtained the way the Vikings got many things, as tribute exacted from a subject people.

A Norwegian merchant of the ninth century named Ottar is described in a history translated and edited by King Alfred of Wessex around 870:

> He was among the chief men in the land . . . . But their riches mainly consist in the tribute which the Lapps pay them. This tribute is of animals' skins, birds' feathers, walrus ivory, and ship ropes that are made from hides of walrus or seals. Every man must pay according to his birth: the most nobly-born must pay 15 marten skins, five reindeer hides, and one bearskin, and ten measures of feathers, a tunicfull of bearskin or otterskin, and two ship's cables made from seal or walrus hide.

To this supply of produce from the north, the Viking trader added other articles desired by his neighbors. These were high-grade iron ore from Sweden, amber—a resinous substance used for beads and ornamental jewelry—and slaves. The slaves were obtained from conquered peoples such as the Irish in the west and the Slavs in the east. There was no ban against the sale of slaves in Christian countries, provided the slaves themselves were not Christians. If they were, the Vikings kept them for their own use.

What did the Vikings want in return for what they had to offer? Principally gold and silver, especially the latter, which they valued highly. The Viking era is sometimes called the Silver Age of Scandinavia. Also, for all their crudities, the Vikings were fond of luxuries and personal adornments. They sought choice wines and studded weaponry from France, glassware from the Rhineland, oriental silks and spices from Arabia, fine fabrics, dyes, and jewelry from the south and east.

To facilitate this interchange of goods, the Vikings established a number of trading centers in the Northlands, among them Kaupang in southern Norway, Birka on Lake Malar in Sweden, and Hedeby in Denmark. These cities were protected by earthen ramparts from possible attack, for the Vikings of one country were not shy about raiding Viking cities in other countries if they felt it would be worth their while. Within the ramparts, turf-walled booths were built as shops or stores where a trader could display his wares and transact his business. Here came men such as Ottar from Norway, merchants from Byzantium, and Arabs from the Mediterranean.

Coins from almost all countries of the Christian and Muslim world have been found in the ruins of these cities. They give testimony to the many nationalities that traded with the Vikings. In those times coins were not regarded as currency in the modern sense. They were pieces of precious metal valued solely by their weight. They were often sliced up like pies to achieve the necessary worth, just as if, today, one cut a fifty-cent piece in half to obtain a quarter.

These market cities also became centers for craftsmen,

who created saleable articles from the raw materials arriving from the north. Thus reindeer antlers were carved into combs, pins, and handles for knives. Walrus tusks became ivory figurines. Beads and ornaments were fashioned from amber. Soapstone was carved into bowls. Glass blowers contributed brightly colored beads. Cloth was woven, and metal fashioned into jewelry.

Always over these peaceful pursuits hung the threat of piratical attack. While the towns were protected, the sea lanes were not. Therefore trading vessels often sailed in convoys, with armed ships to protect them. A single longboat headed for market was a vulnerable pirate target. An 870 account by a missionary named Anskar sailing from Hedeby to Birka relates:

> Halfway across they came upon pirates. And although the merchants who were traveling with them defended themselves manfully and were at first victorious, nevertheless in a second onslaught they were beaten and overwhelmed by the pirates, who robbed them of their ships and all they possessed. It was with great difficulty that they got to land and saved their lives. They had to leave behind the kingly gifts [from the French Emperor] which they had meant to bring to Sweden. They saved only a few petty objects which they could carry with them as they jumped overboard. Among other things they lost almost 40 books which had been meant for the Holy Service, and which fell into the robbers' hands.

Of course, Viking trade was not limited to the local markets near or on the Baltic Sea. Viking merchants ranged far overseas—to the west, to the British Isles, and south to the Mediterranean, the Black and the Caspian seas. Later, when Greenland and Iceland became settled, these countries were added to the commercial itinerary, and such items as wheat and lumber, which these barren islands sorely needed, became Viking exports.

The ships used for this traffic were the relatively light and capacious knorrs, not the longboats, which were used for raiding. The western traffic was never great and was often carried on by individual merchants with a single boat. It was tremendously important, however, to the otherwise isolated Vikings in Greenland and Iceland.

By far the most important trade routes lay to the east—via the Baltic Sea and the Russian rivers—and these were the exclusive province of the Swedish Vikings, the most trade-minded of the Norsemen. Merchant adventurers pursued the Dnieper down to Constantinople, establishing the market cities of Novgorod and Kiev en route. By a treaty concluded with the Byzantine emperor in 911 they were allowed to set up their own trading post outside Constantinople, but could enter the city only at appointed times.

A still more important trade route was the Volga River, leading past the cities of Bulgar and Itil to the Caspian Sea, and on south by camel train to Baghdad. Down the Volga came furs, hides, and slaves, to be exchanged with the Arabs for oriental silks and spices, jewelry and silver.

Though these eastern riverways could accommodate the

smaller clinker-built vessels that the Vikings normally used, the merchants often preferred the even smaller dugouts of the natives. Hollowed out from single trees, these boats were more or less made to order by the Slavs and sold to the Vikings as they arrived with their cargos from the north. Being small, the dugouts were easy to maneuver, especially in such hazards as the Dnieper River rapids.

One Byzantine emperor, Constantine Porphyrogenitus, was also something of a historian. He apparently took a great interest in what these traders from the north endured to reach his city. His description of the first of seven cataracts in the granite gorges, written in 950, is quoted by historian Jacqueline Simpson as follows:

> In the middle of it there are high sheer rocks, which look like islands. When the water reaches them and crashes against them it causes a loud and terrifying tumult as it crashes down. Therefore the Rus do not dare sail between them, but lay their boats alongside the banks before this point and make the people go up on shore, though they leave the cargo on board. Then they walk into the water naked, testing the bottom with their feet so as not to stumble over stones. At the same time they thrust the boat forward with poles, many of them

at the bows, many amidships, and others at the stern. With all these precautions they wade through the edge of these first rapids, close along the bank. As soon as they have passed them, they take the rest of the crew on board, and go on their way by boat.

Some of the other cataracts were not so easily conquered. The emperor writes:

> At the fourth great rapids . . . they all put into the bank with their vessel, and the men whose task it is to keep guard disembark. These guards are necessary because of the Patzinaks [native pirates] who are always lurking in ambush. The rest of them take their goods out of the canoes and lead their slaves, fettered in chains, for six miles over dry land, till they have passed beyond the rapids. After this they transport their boats past the rapids, and then put them back on the river, load their baggage in, get in themselves, and go on their way.

Once the trader arrived at his destination, offerings— often of slaughtered animals, sheep, cattle, or fowl—were made to the Viking god who had guided him to safety. Similarly he took no chances on the hopefully successful outcome of his mission. An Arab trader named Ibn Fadlan described the arrival of a Viking merchant at a trading center on the Volga:

> So he goes up to the big figure [pagan idol], flings himself on the ground, and says: "O my Lord, I have come from far off with so many slaves and so many sable skins" (here he counts up all the wares he has brought) . . . . "I pray that you should send me a merchant who has many dinars

and dirhems, who will buy from me as I wish, and will not contradict what I say."

Not all commerce was carried on by way of sea and rivers. In addition to the camel route from the Caspian to Baghdad, short-distance trade was carried on over land. Horses were used for pack animals and for drawing carts and covered wagons similar to early American prairie schooners. The Vikings also had sledges for winter transport over snow or ice, and some of their vehicles could be fitted with either wheels or runners for summer and winter travel.

Their roads were primitive, but the building of essential bridges was regarded as the responsibility and honored privilege of local chiefs and merchants. Many such bridges were marked with rune stones dedicating their construction to the memory of an illustrious ancestor or former chieftain.

Viking trade began to die out in the eleventh century, as the Vikings themselves were assimilated in the lands they settled or conquered. But the exchange of goods between Scandinavia and the surrounding, more advanced, countries left a lasting impression on both cultures. Viking life, for one thing, became better furnished with the luxuries of that time. Viking women wore silk instead of coarse wool; Viking men drank vintage wine instead of beer. Homes were more comfortable and pleasant; everyone was better fed. Perhaps that is why, at the end of the eleventh century, the Vikings gave up their wide-scale roving and plundering and began to settle down.

13

The Super-Vikings

In sharp contrast to the Vikings who pursued the peaceful arts of trade were the societies or groups of Vikings dedicated solely to the arts of war. In a sense such groups were super-warriors, bound by their common skill and bravery, and pledged to one another by strict oaths of loyalty. They were not interested in land conquests. They were strictly fighters, and ferocious ones at that, and they went to fight where the promise of reward was greatest.

Such was a remarkable, somewhat legendary society known in the tenth century as the Jomsborg Vikings or Jomsvikings.

According to the *Jomsviking Saga* the organization was founded by King Harald Gormsson of Denmark in the year 960. Harald wanted a well-garrisoned fortress on the Baltic to protect his trade routes from pirates and from the hostile people, mostly Slavs, on the south shore of that sea. He had a massive citadel built at the mouth of the Oder River in the Slavic territory known as Wendland (now a part of northern Germany). An artificial harbor was dug, capable of holding 360 ships and protected by great iron doors. Over this entrance rose a mighty arch surmounted by catapults with which to hurl rocks at approaching warships. On the land side, earthen bulwarks completed the citadel's defense.

The stronghold, known as Jomsborg, was garrisoned by Danish Vikings recruited for their size, strength, and fighting skill. In time these Jomsborg Vikings came to regard themselves as a special breed, a knighthood of super-Vikings, owing allegiance to no one but themselves. The laws of the society were very strict. No women were allowed inside the fortress. No man under sixteen or over fifty was accepted. All were pledged to strict obedience and loyalty, to avenge one another's death, never to flinch from danger or utter a word of fear. No individual could leave the citadel for more than three days at a time.

In time the Jomsvikings became more ruthless and terrifying than the pirates they were supposed to exterminate. They roved the Baltic Sea for loot, which they divided equally among themselves. They became the terror of the Viking world, feared even by their fellow Norsemen.

They were extremely proud of their weapons, of their ships, and of their personal appearance. The hilts of the

Jomsvikings' swords were studded with jewels. Their arms were adorned with golden bracelets. Their ships were the swiftest in the Baltic Sea, with high shielded walls for protection in sea battles.

Their lives were dedicated to fighting, and they did not always care who their enemies were. They often hired out as mercenaries to the highest bidder, and would ally themselves at different times with Swedes, Danes, or Norwegians. Says the *Jomsviking Saga*, "They went out and made war in different countries, got high renown and were looked on as the greatest warriors."

The Jomsvikings' recklessness and daring are illustrated by a famous incident.

When King Harald died, his successor, Svein Forkbeard, invited the Jomsborg Vikings under their chieftain Sigvaldi to visit Denmark and to attend a banquet in the late king's honor. Wine was served liberally at the feast. Under its influence the visitors and their hosts sought to outdo each other with extravagant boasting. Svein Forkbeard announced that he would be the first Viking to conquer England. Whereupon Sigvaldi, not to be outdone, boasted that he and his Jomsvikings would shortly conquer Norway and bring King Haakon to his knees.

The next morning, in the light of sobriety, the Jomsvikings were appalled at the rash promise of Sigvaldi. But a promise was not to be ignored. They would have to conquer the kingdom of Norway to preserve their honor. And if they were to take King Haakon by surprise, before he learned of their reckless vow, they would have to act at once.

This they did. With a fleet of 60 longboats they sailed from Denmark up the coast of Norway, stopping for provisions on the way. From a peasant farmer they learned that King Haakon, with only a handful of ships, was hiding in a narrow cliff-encircled arm of the sea known as Jorundfjord. Here he could easily be trapped.

But when they swept into Jorundfjord the Jomsvikings discovered that King Haakon had been warned of their approach and was well prepared. Instead of a handful of ships he had assembled a fleet of 180, outnumbering Sigvaldi's forces by three to one. It was the Jomsvikings who had sailed into a trap.

True to tradition the Jomsborg Vikings never flinched. Though the odds were hopelessly against them, they ploughed into the enemy fleet. Ship clashed against ship and Viking swords against Viking shields in one of the fiercest naval battles of that century. One by one the Jomsborg ships went down, sliced and hacked by a superior foe. The surviving vessels were forced to retreat. The captured Jomsvikings were hauled ashore and beheaded one by one, "showing great bravery as they faced death."

Defeat called for revenge, and the revenge was slow but sweet. Ten years later King Olaf of Norway sought to make a treaty with the Jomsborg Vikings. He daringly visited the citadel with his fleet to suggest that they join forces against their common enemies, the Danes and Swedes.

The Jomsvikings professed to favor this idea. They detained Olaf at the citadel to discuss it, meanwhile making plans of their own.

They knew that outside the fortress lay a combined Danish and Swedish fleet, hoping to catch Olaf as he returned home. Now, at the citadel, a number of Jomsvikings boarded his ships, to act (they said) as pilots in the unfamiliar waters. The spurious pilots led Olaf's ships directly into the arms of the waiting Danish and Swedish longboats, which dashed the Norwegian fleet to pieces.

Foreseeing his capture and disgrace, King Olaf leaped overboard and was never seen again. He was a strong swimmer, and though some thought he had drowned, others believed he had reached shore to renew life under a different name and in disguise. Many were the legends that sprang up about him, and he was reportedly seen in many countries from Italy to England.

As the Jomsvikings grew more confident and daring, they took their warships far afield under the leadership of Thorkel, Sigvaldi's brother. They plundered the south of England, attacked and pillaged London, sacked Canterbury, and murdered the archbishop there. They finally accepted a bribe from King Aethelred of England to leave the country in peace.

The Jomsvikings were becoming such a menace to the other Scandinavian powers that the other powers decided they had to be crushed regardless of the cost. It took King Magnus Olafsson of Norway to accomplish this forbidding task. Olafsson mustered all the available warships in Norway and Denmark and sailed against Jomsborg in 1043. He successfully stormed the citadel, set fire to its wooden barracks, and in hand-to-hand combat slaughtered the defending Vikings. The few he captured alive were beheaded on the spot. Thus ended, by fire and sword, the 80-year reign of the Jomsvikings on the Baltic.

A similar order of super-Vikings, organized at the end of the tenth century in the Byzantine capital of Constantinople, was known as the Varangian Guard. The Dnieper River Vikings who founded the Russian state never suc-

ceeded in conquering Constantinople. But they so impressed the Byzantine emperor, Basil II, with their courage and ferocity that he hired them for his personal guard and later for his private army.

Known as the "axe-bearing barbarians," the Varangian Guards were selected, like the Jomsvikings, for their size, strength, and skill with weapons. Because they spoke a different language, the emperor considered them safe from the intrigues of his often rebellious subjects. The Guards were bound to the emperor and to one another by oaths of loyalty, and these oaths were fortified by excellent pay.

The Varangian Guard was the most privileged group in Constantinople. The members dressed in elegant white tunics with gold belts and gold armbands. They were paid in gold, and once a year their officers were allowed to walk through the emperor's chamber and carry off as many precious articles as they could hold.

In time the Guard became a magnet for all Russian Vikings, for it offered a man a chance to win distinction, wealth, and glory while stationed at the emperor's palace. They would fight anywhere, against any enemy, for the promise of reward. Although their exact number is unrecorded, it is known that a select band of 6,000 Vikings from Kiev arrived in Constantinople in 988 to form the nucleus of this prestigious group.

One of the early leaders, and some say founder, of the Varangian Guard was "that most glorious prince of adventurers," Harald Hardradi. The Viking Harald came to

Constantinople from Norway in the year 1034 with 500 of his followers. He was shortly hailed in the Byzantine capital as "King of Varangians." The emperor, then Michael IV, anxious to test Harald's prowess, sent him and his troops to fight the Arabs in Asia Minor. It was not usual for Vikings to fight at long distance from their ships, but the Varangian Guard was essentially an infantry unit rather than a force of seaborne warriors.

By his own boast, Harald conquered more than 80 Arab strongholds. He surrounded Jerusalem, then under Arab control, and exacted permission for all Christians to visit its holy shrines at will. He was then sent by the emperor to conquer Sicily. On this Mediterranean island he overcame several fortified cities by a number of ruses.

In one instance he dug a tunnel from a dry river bed into the center of a citadel, and up into the dining hall of the palace. His men rose from the floor to surprise the defending Sicilians in the middle of their evening meal.

In another instance, Harald's men made no attempt to storm the city. They camped outside the walls and engaged in seemingly harmless games to pass the time. The city's defenders, becoming curious, came out through the gates to watch the games. Whereupon Harald's forces dropped their playful charade, seized their weapons, and charged through the undefended gates.

It is largely because of Harald Hardradi and the Varangian Guard that the Vikings left their footprints on the Mediterranean countries of Greece and Italy as well as in eastern Europe. They left their marks in the Aegean islands, Asia Minor, the Caucasus, Sicily, and Bulgaria. After his victories over the Bulgars, Harald returned to Constantinople to receive many honors for "having achieved greatly."

By this time Harald evidently considered himself a man of power and influence in Constantinople. For when the Emperor Michael IV was succeeded by a far less acceptable ruler, Harald himself led the popular revolt that overwhelmed the palace. When the new emperor and his followers were taken prisoner, Harald personally gouged out their eyes.

Next, Harald left the Varangian Guard around 1042 to return to Scandinavia where he sought to depose his nephew Magnus who was king of Norway. The rivalry between them was settled by an agreement to share the throne. Shortly thereafter Magnus died and Harald became the sole, undisputed king.

Though the Varangian Guard continued for at least 20 years after Harald's return to Norway, it began to decline after 1066 when many of its members enlisted in William the Conqueror's expedition against England. In time, only legend kept alive the heroic feats of the two great societies of super-warriors, the Jomsvikings and the Varangian Guard.

14

The Last Great Days in England

His name was Olaf Tryggvason, known more simply as Olaf, and he was hailed in Norway as "the greatest Viking warrior of his time." He was also a prince in line for the Norwegian throne. Tall, strong, and handsome, he had won great renown on Viking expeditions in the Baltic Sea and Russia. And he was to be the first of three great kings who led the Vikings to their supreme moment in history, the conquest and rule of England.

At the end of the tenth century, Olaf heard reports of the weak king ruling England. This king was called Aethelred the Unready, and his nickname was deserved. Since the start of his reign, bands of Vikings had raided the English coast at will. Olaf decided he would lead an expedition to see just how unready the king was, for England though weak was still wealthy.

So in 991 began the second invasion of England after years of hard-won peace. Olaf's forces were not great, only 93 ships with perhaps 5,000 men. But his navy included such formidable vessels as the famed *Long Serpent*, a giant ship whose appearance alone struck terror in the hearts of beholders. And his men were hand-picked, some of them from the famous Jomsborg society. As for Olaf's craftiness at leading men in battle, no man was his equal.

The Viking armada, with raven standards flying from the mastheads, bucked across the stormy North Sea to the estuary of the Blackwater River northeast of London. The Vikings scrambled ashore near Maldon, making their camp on an island, with the river on one side and the tideswept causeway on the other. It was there that the English came to meet them, led by one of Aethelred's earls named Brihtnoth.

The two armies faced one another across the causeway, hurling challenges and insults. The Vikings shouted to their opponents:

"Send quickly rings for your safety: it is better for you to buy off with tribute this storm of spears, than that we should share the bitter war. . . . We will with gold set up a truce. . . . We will go abroad with the tribute, and sail the sea, and be at peace with you."

The English remained unmoved. It was many years since they had faced a Viking army, long enough to forget the terror of Viking arms.

"Brihtnoth spoke and grasped his shield, brandished the slender spear, and, wrathful and unwavering, gave him answer: 'Hearest thou, rover, what this people saith? They will give you in tribute spears, and deadly darts, and swords. . . .' "

While they were taunting one another, the tide crept in over the causeway, making it difficult for the Vikings to reach their foe. Then came one of those sporting arrangements that often accompanied war in that romantic period. The Vikings asked that they be allowed to cross over the causeway and arrange their men for battle unmolested. Then the two sides could fight on equal terms.

The request was gallantly granted, to the misfortune of the English. For once on high ground the Vikings fell upon their foe with such fury and such disregard for loss of life that Brihtnoth's troops were literally cut to pieces. It was the worst defeat, at the hands of any enemy, that England had suffered in 100 years.

Aethelred made no attempt to avenge this defeat by force. Instead he fell back on the cowardly expedient of offering Olaf a danegeld, or bribe, of 10,000 pounds of silver if the Viking force would leave England in peace. He furthermore offered Olaf's men all the provisions they might need so long as they were on English soil. It bought the English time, but it paved the way for future Viking invasions.

Olaf pretended to accept the offer, but he had no intention of leaving England in peace. He simply moved his operations to the north of England, where he raided and plundered for three fruitful years. At the end of that period

he was joined by another great Viking leader, Svein Forkbeard, King of Denmark. Svein brought a fleet of 94 ships
to add to Olaf's navy and together they sailed up the
Thames to London and beyond, burning and plundering
as they went. This resulted in Aethelred paying another
danegeld of 16,000 pounds to persuade the Vikings to withdraw.

This time Olaf sailed back to Norway where he succeeded to the throne, later losing his kingdom in a naval
battle in the Baltic with the Danes and Swedes. It was
during that encounter that, as previously mentioned, Olaf
jumped overboard and was never seen again.

Svein Forkbeard continued, without his partner, to
harass the vacillating English. The *Saxon Chronicle* records
that in the year 999:

> The Danes came round into the Thames, and up along
> the Medway to Rochester. And the Kentish force came
> against them, and they fought sharply. But, alas, that they
> all too quickly gave way and fled, because they had not
> the support that they should have had. And the Danes held
> the field; and then took horses and rode whithersoever they
> would, and ruined almost all West Kent.

King Aethelred desperately gathered together all the
ships he could find in the vicinity of London, and added
a makeshift navy to his troops on land. But as always no
navy could match the Vikings' skill in seaborne battle.

> And ever they let the host of their foes increase; and ever
> the English withdrew from the sea, and the Danes followed

them up. And then, in the end, neither the navy nor the land-force came to anything, save the toil of the people, and waste of money, and encouragement of the enemy.

As usual, Aethelred ended up by pacifying Svein's Vikings with another danegeld, the third he had paid in less than ten years, this one of 24,000 pounds. For the Vikings this had become a profitable routine. The payment of danegeld supported the army until it was ready to attack again and exact another danegeld. England was paying handsomely for its own destruction.

But Aethelred smarted under these payments, and when he heard of a plot upon his life he lost his reason. In a fit of deranged fury he committed the most outrageous act of his regime. He ordered the massacre of all Danes in the south of England, most of them now simply peaceful settlers and farmers. The abominable deed was executed on St. Brice's Day of 1002, and among the victims was Svein's sister Gunnhild.

The consequence was easy to foresee. When Svein heard of this atrocity, he descended on England with the massed swords of all the Vikings under his command, and launched a five-year reign of terror that had no equal in Viking history. City after city was sacked and burned, churches and monasteries plundered. All in the way of this march of death were slain. The English were so completely ter-rorized that 36,000 pounds of tribute was paid to Svein to discontinue the ruthless slaughter.

With this enormous booty Svein returned to his throne

in Denmark. But he still smoldered with anger against England. It was not long before he sent one of his lieutenants, Thorkel the Tall, a Jomsborg Viking, to continue the harassment of Britain, with special instructions to capture the city of London. This was easy to command, but almost impossible to do. London was protected by a bridge across the Thames, heavily fortified against invaders.

Thorkel undertook to destroy the bridge. He built roofs over a number of his longboats so that his Vikings would be protected from missiles hurled from above. The boats were then rowed up to the bridge, where great ropes were thrown around the supporting piles. With this accomplished, the Vikings rowed downstream with the current, muscles straining to the utmost, till the piles were uprooted and the bridge came tumbling down. From this incident comes the famous children's nursery chant, "London Bridge Is Falling Down."

Thorkel's forces then proceeded up the river to ravage what had once been the Danelaw, or territory of their fellow Danes, so many of whom had been slaughtered on St. Brice's Day. The wretched and terrified King Aethelred was unable to stem the bloody tide, and again fell back on offering the Vikings tribute to withdraw. The amount this time was a record 48,000 pounds. But in return for this sum, Thorkel agreed to come over to the English side with 45 of his longboats, and help Aethelred repel future Viking raids.

However, if Aethelred thought he was buying peace and

security, he was much mistaken. "For soon came the great Svein himself, wrathful and jealous, to prove his might by a greater achievement than that of his treacherous lieutenant." This was no vengeful attack for plunder. Svein had now vowed to make himself king of England.

Aethelred and Thorkel took refuge in London, and braced themselves for the attack. But Svein bypassed London. He had no need to take the city when all of England lay open to him. He traveled by boat and horse from the English Channel to the Irish Sea, rallying to his side the English people who had lost their faith in Aethelred. Soon all England was ready to declare him king. Aethelred, seeing the writing on the wall, slipped out of London and fled with his fleet to Normandy in France.

For the first time in history a Viking king ruled England. But this triumph was not to last, for Svein died within a year. His rightful successor was his son Canute. But Canute was only eighteen years old. He was something of an unknown quantity. The English saw this as a chance to regain the throne. They sent a message to Aethelred to return from France, warning him, however, that he had better prove himself a stronger ruler than he had to date.

Canute, for his part, sailed to Denmark to gain reinforcements for his role as king. He was greatly aided when Thorkel deserted Aethelred and rejoined the Danes. When Canute returned in 1015 to assert his claim to the English throne, he sailed up the Thames to embattled London and once again laid siege to the town. Unable to scale its fortifi-

cations he ordered his Vikings to dig a trench around the
city, and by this ingenious method made the Londoners his
prisoners.

The English fought, at times gallantly, to save their
kingdom. But they were often betrayed by leaders in their
ranks, who shamefully fled from the scene of battle, or went
over with their troops to Canute's forces. When Aethelred
died, his son and successor, Edmund Ironside, strove to
continue the defense of England and even agreed to share
the country with Canute. But the deal was never consum-
mated. Edmund died suddenly and left Canute in undisputed possession of the throne.

This was the Vikings' finest hour in their long and
fluctuating history. A Viking king ruled all of England.
Viking armies controlled the country, and a Viking fleet
controlled the seas.

Canute turned out to be one of the greater kings of
history. He changed, in character and actions, from a Viking pirate to a wise and compassionate ruler. To prove that
he meant to rule by wisdom, not by might, he paid his army
and sent it back to Denmark. He then rebuilt the churches
and monasteries that the Vikings had destroyed. He em-
braced the Christian faith and encouraged all his people to
do likewise.

Conversion of the Vikings to Christianity took place
often in the eleventh century. But it did not mean an immediate change in Viking character; it meant simply that
they accepted the customs of the countries they had

conquered. And in time it led to a more settled and less violent way of life.

Canute was not only king of England, he was also king of Denmark and Norway, so that the three countries formed a confederacy under his rule. In time Scotland joined this group, along with the Atlantic Islands. Canute's empire rivaled any that existed in the Middle Ages.

Yet he was a scholarly and humble king. He did not wish to be idolized or worshiped as a god. There is a familiar legend that Canute invited his courtiers to accompany him to the seashore, and there commanded the waves to be stilled. When the surf continued to break at his feet, Canute turned to his followers and counseled them that no man, not even he, had superhuman powers.

When Canute died in 1035 his kingdom was partitioned among three sons, none of whom was fit to rule. As a result the Danish dynasty in England lasted only seven years, after which the throne reverted to a son of Aethelred, Edward the Confessor.

But the Vikings made one last attempt at taking over England. In 1066 Harald Hardradi, founder of the Varangian Guard and now king of Norway, invaded the country with intent to seize the throne. Though over fifty years of age, Harald was still a formidable warrior, deserving the title ascribed to him, "Thunderbolt of the North." He brought his fleet inland as far as York, where his men disembarked to continue their invasion on foot. At Stamford Bridge they were surprised by a sizable English army under King Harold. The Vikings sought to make a bargain, and asked what King Harold of England would offer King Harald of Norway in return for peace. They were told:

"To Harald of Norway, Harold of England will give seven feet of English ground, or as much more as he may be taller than other men."

The battle which followed was stubbornly fought, and ended when Harald of Norway received an arrow in his throat, and thereby won his seven feet of English ground. He was the last Viking chief to die on English soil—or, almost the last. For at the same time that the Battle of Stamford Bridge was fought, another mighty force was poised on the shores of Kent to strike for the throne of England. William the Conqueror was not, strictly speaking, a Viking. But he came from Normandy, the Viking-held province of France, and so most surely Viking blood flowed in his veins. In the Battle of Hastings, which decided England's fate forever, Viking blood and Viking spirit weighed heavily in favor of the Norman victors.

15

Land of Ice and Fire

By the middle of the ninth century the Vikings had ranged east, south, and west, invading the neighboring countries of Russia, France, England, and Ireland. They had conquered and settled in the islands north of Scotland: the Hebrides, the Orkneys, the Shetlands, and the Faroes.

There was only one way left for them to go: farther west across the broad Atlantic. In this direction lay Iceland, Greenland, and America. The Vikings did not yet know of these places. But they were soon to find out.

Because the long coastline of Norway faces west, it was natural for the Norwegian Vikings to set out in that direction. They may have first heard about Iceland from the Irish when they all but took possession of that country. Many priests and devout Christians in Ireland had sought to escape the pagan Viking scourge by fleeing to Iceland. News of their new-found refuge may have leaked back to the Viking conquerors.

In an age of remarkable sea voyages, this flight of the Irish to Iceland is as remarkable as any. If they sailed almost due north, it was 1,200 miles across the open sea. Or they may have reached Iceland via the Shetland and Faroe islands. But in open boats, often with only a single pair of oars and no compass to guide them, the fugitive Irish must have relied heavily on faith and courage. Even so, they found no peace. As soon as the Vikings began to arrive, they took to their boats and disappeared. No one knows for certain where the Irish went on fleeing Iceland.

Sailing from Norway as the Vikings did, the voyage to Iceland was fairly easy. On a clear summer day one could sail due west to the Shetland Islands, then northwest to the Faroes, almost without losing sight of land.

From the Faroes west to Iceland lay 400 miles of open water. But the currents are favorable, for here the Gulf Stream, in its long sweep across the North Atlantic, pushes north to almost encircle the southerly shores of Iceland. It not only helped to carry the Vikings in the way they wanted to go, but its warm waters tended to keep the coast of Iceland free of ice, despite its forbidding name.

Nevertheless the Vikings first came upon Iceland more or less by accident, around the year 860. Credit might be divided between two men, Gardar and Naddod. Gardar was sailing to the Hebrides to claim some land that his wife had inherited. Blown off course, he spent the summer on an island he named "Snowland." Naddod was sailing to the Faroes but was driven by storms, like Gardar, to the shores of "Snowland." Both men returned home with tempting descriptions of a land of verdant pastures and abundant game and fish.

Their stories inspired a Viking named Loki to investigate this new land with a view toward settling there. Loki used ravens to guide him to his destination. As he made the long crossing from the Faroe Islands he released one raven, which promptly flew back home. Later Loki released another raven, which circled overhead for a while and then returned to the ship. Finally, a third raven was released. This one flew north and disappeared. Loki knew that this meant it had found land, and he followed its course to his destination.

Loki took a dim view of this new land, which he renamed Iceland. And in some respects, indeed, it must have looked like the surface of the moon. Except for some fertile pastureland and scrubby forests along the shore, the island was a desert of rocky mountains and glaciers. It was scarred with the craters of volcanoes, and plumes of steam rose from its hot springs. Four fifths of it was a land of ice and fire. Even today, when Iceland is an independent republic of 200,000 Viking descendants, 80 percent of the island is uninhabited.

Loki spent one winter there by choice, to see if it were fit to live in, and another by accident, when his ship was wrecked on setting sail for Norway. He finally returned home with a discouraging report about the island. It was not suitable for a Viking and his family, Loki said. But one of his group named Thorolf gave a very different, and encouraging, account. He reported that the island contained pastureland so rich that every blade of grass dripped butter, whereupon his fellows gave him the name of Thorolf Butter.

Apparently the Norwegian Vikings believed Thorolf more than Loki. Following Loki's voyage the real settlement of Iceland began. The first to emigrate and settle there were two foster brothers, Leif and Ingolf. They were great troublemakers in Norway, involved in one scrape after another until it seemed wise for them to leave the country. But they needed money for ships and provisions. So Leif, according to the Iceland sagas, "went harrying in Ireland . . . he harried far and wide, winning great wealth there and taking ten slaves captive."

With Leif's ill-gained wealth the brothers fitted out two vessels and set sail for Iceland. The ships were undoubtedly knorrs, which were stouter and roomier than the longboats, with high sides to protect them from the stormy seas. In these sturdy vessels the brothers were able to take their wives and children, sacks and kegs of salted meat and fish, and a few livestock to begin their farms.

As they neared the shores of Iceland, the brothers resorted to a Viking custom of determining the place to land. They had brought with them their "high-seat pillars" which marked the place of honor in the great hall of their homes, a sort of throne for the master of the house. These pillars had great personal significance, for they were symbols of the Viking's rank. Now they threw these pillars overboard, to follow where they drifted. Ingolf's pillars came ashore on the southern tip of Iceland. Leif's pillars landed farther up the western coast where now stands the capital city of Reykjavík.

Leif's desire to take his ten slaves with him proved his undoing. The slaves, alone now with their master and his small band of followers, rose up in mutiny, killed Leif and his crew, and made their women captive. Ingolf soon knew something was wrong when he had no word from his brother. He followed Leif's route and found the body. Thereupon he pursued the slaves, slaughtered every one, and freed the captive women. On this bloody note the settlement of Iceland began. Ingolf remained on his brother's estate, to be followed there and all along the west coast by scores of Viking settlers from Norway.

The emigration from Norway to Iceland was prompted not only by the search for land. True, good territory was becoming scarce in Norway. Ambitious men were driven to look overseas for open land on which to raise their crops and graze their cattle. Iceland was not a good place to raise crops, but was excellent for dairy farming, which became the country's leading occupation.

Another reason for the flood of emigrants to Iceland between 870 and 930 was the tyrannical rule of Harald Fairhair, king of Norway. Vikings were by nature an independent lot. They resented any discipline imposed upon them, and did not easily yield to authority. When King Harald imposed strict rules and stricter penalties for breaking rules, they pulled up stakes and headed for the new-found island overseas.

It was somewhat like the opening and settlement of the American West, albeit with families arriving not by covered wagon but by open ship. They brought as many of their belongings with them as the boats could carry, and home-steaded on the most promising land that they could find. With them came many outlaws barred from Norway, super-Vikings who believed in taking what they wanted by force. It was a new land, with all the lawless violence of the frontier.

By 930 the population of Iceland had reached 30,000. It did not grow much larger until modern times, because there was not enough room. Virtually all the habitable land was occupied. This was the level strip between the ice-capped mountains and the sea, along the south and west coasts. A man could own as much land as he could walk around in a day, which meant that the estates were large and isolated from one another.

What government there was in Iceland rested on the *godi*, or leading chieftain of a district. The godi was also the high priest of the pagan gods, Thor and Odin. It was his responsibility to build a chapel to these gods, to conduct services, and also to settle matters of dispute among his people.

To settle disputes was difficult if not impossible. If a man

did not like the decision of his chief, he simply shifted his allegiance to another godi. Personal vengeance took the place of justice. Duels were frequent. An eye for an eye became the true law of the land.

Plainly a national government was needed. It was natural that this should be modeled after the *things*, or local assemblies of Scandinavia. In 930 an "All Things," or Althing was established. It was a gathering of all the chieftains and their people to make laws, settle disputes, and pass judgment on offenders.

The Althing met for two weeks every summer at Thingvellir, or "Plain of the Thing," a five-mile-long meadow about 30 miles from Reykjavík. The meetings were not devoted entirely to matters of law. They were great festive occasions where jugglers and musicians performed, contests and dancing were held, and people met informally to gossip and exchange news and stories.

No system of government is perfect and the Althing was far from perfect. There was no police force. The Althing could make laws but it could not enforce them. It could pass judgment on offenders, but it could not bring them to justice. It was up to the offended party to avenge himself, which resulted in widespread duels and bloodshed.

However, establishment of the Althing, despite its faults, is a landmark in history. It marked Iceland as the first democratic republic in the western world, and the Althing lasted from 930 to 1798, more than 850 years.

Under the Althing, Christianity came to pagan Iceland. Though the country was independent, it had to rely on

Norway for many basic provisions such as grain, lumber, iron utensils, and weapons. This required staying in the favor of King Olaf Tryggvason of Norway, himself a convert to Christianity. The king decided to make Iceland Christian to bind it closer to his throne.

Olaf sent a number of missionaries to Iceland, but these missionaries acted in typical Viking fashion. They smashed the idols, wrecked the temples, and tried to win converts by force. The Icelanders soon had enough of them and drove them back to Norway.

This so enraged King Olaf that he too fell back on old Viking tactics. He threatened to massacre all the Icelanders he could find in Norway if Iceland did not accept the faith. When news of this threat reached Iceland, a wholesale conversion to Christianity took place, and in the year 1000 the Althing made it the religion of the country.

But conversion by force is not apt to be sincere. Though the Icelanders accepted baptism, it was more for the sake of keeping peace with Norway than an act of faith. They continued to practice their pagan rites in private for many years.

From Iceland came many of the written documents that provide invaluable knowledge of the Viking era. Chief among these are 120 sagas, or stories passed down from generation to generation. The sagas are a proud and unique Viking contribution to the world's literature. More than history, they have a style and tradition of their own. They are graced with warmth and a sense of poetry that seem strange coming from a barbaric people, but these qualities may be attributed to the Viking spirit, which glorified the past and romanticized the struggles and achievements of ancestors.

Some sagas narrate the exploits of great Viking leaders, others relate the history of distinguished families, and still others deal with great events in Viking history, with voyages, battles, and discoveries. Whatever the subject, they are thrilling tales of adventure, and make exciting reading even today. In addition to the sagas, there were also Icelandic historians such as Snorri Sturluson, and *skalds*, or poets, who recorded Viking deeds in verse.

Iceland became part of Norway in 1264, was transferred to the Danish crown in 1380, and became an independent republic in 1944. It has one of the highest literacy rates in the world. Almost everyone in the country can read and write. The publication of new books per capita is 20 times that of the United States. It seems that the rich literary heritage of the Viking age has continued down to the present day.

There are three reasons why Iceland is of prime importance in Viking history. One was its early democratic government based on the Althing. Another was its phenomenal literature, which tells so much about the Vikings. And the third was this: Lying directly on the seapath to Greenland and America, Iceland was the jumping off place for the exploration of these countries. It was an essential stepping-stone to the crowning achievement of the Viking age, the movement west across the North Atlantic and the discovery of America.

16

~~~~~~

Adventures of Eric the Red and Bjarni

Eric the Red is a name that calls to mind the sound of sea and wind and clashing battleaxes. For Eric was one of the most adventurous of the Vikings. With his sons he fostered the great voyages westward to Greenland and America. The red hair that gave him his name was a clue to his ungovernable temper.

Eric had violence and daring in his blood. His father had been outlawed from Norway "because of some killings," the sagas briefly state. About the year 963 the family went to Iceland to settle on one of the few remaining strips of habitable land.

Shortly after his father died Eric also became involved in "some killings." The story is that Eric's slaves caused a landslide that smothered the farm of his neighbor and killed the inhabitants. Landslides were common in the shale and gravel hills of Iceland, so it might have been an accident. But the neighbor's relatives slaughtered the slaves in retaliation, prompting Eric to get even by killing two of the neighbor's kin in a battle of revenge. As a result, Eric was exiled from Iceland for a period of three years.

Where could he go? No country that he knew would have him.

But there was a possible solution. The Iceland Vikings still traded with the British Isles. And from the people of Ireland who had fled the Viking scourge came word of a land to the west, which they called Greater Ireland. From an Irish skald, or poem, came the lines:

> To seaward, to the northwest,
> Frost and cold
> And fearful wonders.

Moreover, some 80 years earlier a Viking named Gunnbjorn had undertaken a voyage of exploration around the great sea adjoining Iceland. He reported having sighted an island or islands far off to the west. Gunnbjorn had not investigated further, and Icelanders had done no more than wonder about this mysterious discovery. Did such land really exist? Was it Greater Ireland? Eric decided he would use his period of banishment to find out.

He entrusted his wife and children to the care of relatives, and fitted out a good-size knorr for the voyage. Some 20 men agreed to go along as crew, for there was much curiosity about this mysterious western land and Iceland was getting overcrowded. They filled the knorr with cattle and chickens for fresh meat on the voyage, and brought along enough grain and water for several months.

The expedition had one advantage. The branch of the Gulf Stream that sweeps around Iceland also bears toward the southern tip of Greenland and continues up the west coast of that island. Once Eric had crossed the Denmark Strait west of Iceland, a three-days' sail with less than a day out of sight of land, he had no trouble finding his way down the Greenland coast to the west shore where the Gulf Stream kept the climate mild and encouraged the growth of grass and scrub.

When Eric reached Greenland he found a fjord, which he named Eric's Fjord, or Ericsfjord, and, true to Viking custom, settled on a small island near its mouth called Eric's Island. He still did not know whether Greenland was inhabited by friends or enemies, and an island offered natural defenses against a surprise attack.

For the next three summers Eric and his men explored this new land, which they found completely uninhabited. Winters they huddled in their solid, compact earthen huts to wait out the cold. It was a raw, wild land that nonetheless suited Eric. The hunting and fishing were good. There were ample fields along the coast for pasturing cattle. A man who settled here could have as much land as he wanted. He would be free to live as he liked.

Before returning to Iceland, the sagas say, Eric "named

the country *Greenland*, for he said that people would be tempted to go there if it had an attractive name." Eric was anxious to settle the land with neighbors of his choosing.

Back in Iceland after his three-year period of banishment, Eric had no trouble interesting others in this new-found country. He himself meant to settle there, and he gathered his wife and children and stocked the boat with all the cattle and provisions, along with household goods, that it could carry. By the time spring came again there were 25 or 35 other ships ready to join the expedition, each crowded with sheep, goats, cattle, and provisions, with as many as 20 to 30 people in each boat.

It seems probable that the ships were dangerously over-loaded because the voyage, which started with such high hopes, suffered many losses. Only 14 vessels of the fleet reached Greenland. What happened to the rest is shrouded in mystery. But there is a clue in a chronicle that refers to the terrors of the "ocean whirl."

> It has the appearance as if all the waves and storms of the ocean had been collected into three heaps out of which three great waves form. These so surround the entire sea that no opening can be seen anywhere; they are higher than lofty mountains and resemble steep overhanging cliffs. In only a few cases have men been known to escape who were upon the sea when such a thing occurred.

At least one historian, Farley Mowat, concludes that the "ocean whirl" was a vast upheaval of the sea caused by an underwater earthquake or an undersea volcano. Certainly such violent disturbances were common in the Greenland Sea. Quite recently a whole new island sprang into existence in the Greenland Sea from a volcanic eruption.

Another explanation might lie in the calving of icebergs on those northern shores. Particularly during the summer great masses of ice detached themselves from the glacial walls and plunged with a mighty roar into the sea, sending tidal waves surging for miles across the ocean. One can easily imagine how the Viking knorrs, sturdily built though they were, would be hopelessly swamped by such a cataclysm.

The 14 ships that reached Greenland were directed each to a separate fjord where the groups could settle without crowding one another. Thus each chieftain had his own small colony. The ritual of claiming land was simple. The chieftain simply walked around the territory that he wanted, carrying a torch and repeating over and over again: "I take this land for my own, for I see no inhabited dwellings hereabouts."

Eric the Red claimed an immense tract on both sides of Ericsfjord. He called this "Brattalid" and there built his home. Like all the chieftains' houses, Eric's was built of sod and stone, there being little wood in Greenland, and the walls were 8 to 12 feet thick to keep out the winter cold. There were no windows, but in the great hall was the customary central fireplace with a hole in the roof to let out smoke and let in light.

That summer and fall the settlers gathered as much wood

as they could for fuel and hunted and fished for food to tide them over until spring. They had also to gather in hay to feed the cattle during winter months. When spring finally came again, the settlers had survived but that was about all. There were few natural resources on the island—no iron with which to make tools, for example; these had to be fashioned from bone. So the islanders had little to trade, little to attract merchant vessels to the new land. They were on their own in a barren isolated world.

One of the Viking chiefs who had followed Eric the Red to Iceland, and later Greenland, was a man named Herjolf. Herjolf had a son in Iceland named Bjarni about whom the sagas say: "Bjarni was a most promising man. Even in his youth he loved seafaring. Soon Bjarni owned a ship and trade goods. He was well off in wealth and stood high in men's esteem."

Bjarni's name should be remembered, for he is an often-neglected hero in the tales of Viking explorations. Bjarni was trading overseas when his father sailed from Iceland. Bjarni came home to an empty house and a message that his father had followed Eric the Red to Greenland. The sagas relate:

> The news came as a shock to Bjarni, and he refused to have his ship unloaded. His crew asked him what he had in mind; he replied that he intended to keep his custom of enjoying his father's hospitality over the winter—"so I want to sail my ship to Greenland, if you are willing to come with me."
> They all replied that they would do what he thought

best. Then Bjarni said, "This voyage of ours will be considered foolhardy, for not one of us has ever sailed the Greenland Sea."

However, they put to sea . . . and sailed for three days until land was lost to sight below the horizon. Then the fair wind failed and northerly winds and fog set in, and for many days they had no idea what their course was.

It seems likely that Bjarni, perhaps following his father's instructions, had started on the direct route from Iceland to Cape Farewell on the southern tip of Greenland. Had the weather remained favorable he would have had no trouble, for he was thirty-four years old and had many years of sea experience behind him.

But a northeast storm in that part of the world is disastrous. It whips the sea into giant waves and charges the air with so much mist and spray that a pilot cannot see beyond his vessel's bow. Furthermore, the Viking ships had shallow keels. This meant that all the time Bjarni was sailing toward the west, his ship was being carried southward by the wind.

When the storm and fog finally lifted, Bjarni must have noticed that the noonday sun stood high overhead. This and the position of the North Star would have told him that he was far south of his intended landing. How far west he was he could not know. He hoisted sail and headed north, sure at least of the need to move in that direction. It wasn't long before the lookout at the masthead sighted land to port, or to the west.

It is likely that this was Newfoundland, and if so this was

the true discovery of America for Newfoundland is separated from the North American mainland by only a very
narrow strait.

Bjarni moved closer to shore to investigate. He saw that
the land was one of low, heavily wooded hills. Yet his father
had said that Greenland was a land of icy mountains, and
few forests. And Bjarni was interested only in reaching
Greenland as soon as possible. Had he gone ashore, he
would have been the first European man to set foot on
North America. But he pressed on, as the sagas relate.

> So they put to sea again, leaving the land on the port
> quarter; and after sailing for two days they sighted land
> once more.
> Bjarni's men asked him if he thought this was Greenland
> yet; he said he did not think this was Greenland, any more
> than the previous one—"for there are said to be huge
> glaciers in Greenland."
> They closed the land quickly and saw that it was flat and
> wooded.

Though his men were eager to go ashore on what was
undoubtedly more of Newfoundland, Bjarni insisted on
holding to sea. He kept on north along the coast for three
more days. Then they sighted a third land, probably Labrador. It was "high and mountainous and topped by a
glacier." Again the men were eager to land, but Bjarni told
them, "No, for this country seems to me to be worthless."

By the position of the sun Bjarni knew he had reached
the latitude of Greenland, meaning that if he sailed due

east he would reach his destination. This he did, and the decision proved correct. He landed almost on his father's doorstep in Herjolfsfjord.

Bjarni was strangely silent about the lands he had discovered. "People thought he had shown great lack of enterprise, since he could tell them nothing about these countries, and he was derided for this." Perhaps he was embarrassed at being blown off course and failing to follow the shortest route to Greenland.

In any event, he gave up seafaring and devoted himself to caring for the farm after his father's death. So Bjarni got no fame or credit for his remarkable voyage to another world. Rather, he left it to another—Eric's son Leif—to become perhaps the best known figure in Viking history, the man who discovered America 500 years before Columbus.

17

Leif the Lucky Discovers America

Though Bjarni may have talked little in public about the new lands he had seen, one of the first things he did on arriving home was to call on Eric the Red at Brattalid. This was only proper. Eric was the principal chieftain of Greenland, almost a local king. He deserved to know of anything that happened to his subjects.

In the great hall around the open fire, Bjarni related his adventures to the aging Eric. Present were Eric's three sons, Thorvald, Thorstein, and Leif. The boys were wide-eyed at these tales of distant lands and storms at sea. Leif especially devoured every word of Bjarni's story, for like his father he was born for seafaring and excitement. In fact, he was ready to set out at once to explore these distant lands of mystery.

But Leif Ericsson was then only fifteen, and his father told him he would have to come of age before tackling such an enterprise. Meanwhile, to keep Leif occupied and to satisfy his restlessness, Eric arranged for the boy to visit Norway and fitted out a ship for this purpose. It would be a good education for Leif to become acquainted with the homeland of his forefathers. And while there he could plead with the new king, Olaf Tryggvason, for trading ships to visit Greenland and to bring articles that the island sorely needed.

Leif was a good-looking youngster, tall and red-haired like his father, and mature for his age. Eric the Red's name would gain him ready acceptance at the king's court, for wasn't Eric the leading chieftain of a land even larger than King Olaf's Norway?

Leif made a good impression on King Olaf, who persuaded the lad to be baptized a Christian. He then sent him back as a missionary to convert the Greenland colony to Christianity, assigning a priest to help him. Before setting sail for the return voyage, Leif filled his ship with lumber, grain, and iron utensils to trade with his fellow Greenlanders.

As Eric's son, Leif had considerable influence on the island and by the year 1000 most of Greenland had accepted the Christian faith. Only Eric the Red refused to be converted and clung to the pagan gods, though his wife built a Christian chapel at Brattalid, the remains of which were only recently discovered.

West
Settlement

Brattalid

L'Anse aux Meadows
NEWFOUNDLAND

On reaching twenty-three, Leif resolved to set out on a voyage of exploration to the western lands. There was much talk of land-seeking among the Greenlanders; the colony was expanding and it needed room. Leif went down to the Herjolf farm where Bjarni's boat had been stored in good condition. With the money obtained from his Norwegian cargo, he bought the ship and persuaded Bjarni to join him on the expedition.

Leif also tried to persuade his father to go with them, hinting that Eric could lead the expedition. Eric reluctantly agreed. But on the ride down to the harbor, Eric injured

NLAND

NORTH
ATLANTIC
OCEAN

ICELAND

Reykjavik

FAROE
ISLANDS

his foot when his horse slipped and threw him to the
ground. Surely this was a warning from the gods! The
Greenland Saga quotes Eric as saying: "It is not my fate to
find more lands than this where we now dwell. You and I
may no longer follow together."

The sagas suggest that Eric may have planned the accident in order to leave Leif on his own. This does not seem
too unlikely because "Leif was a very tall and vigorous man,
a brave fellow to look at, a shrewd man and careful in all
things." He could well look after himself. And his hand-
picked crew of 35 stalwart Greenlanders was loyal and

dependable. Many had sailed with Bjarni on the earlier voyage. Among them was a man called Tyrkir, who had served as Leif's foster father during the period that Eric the Red had been banished from Iceland.

So, on a clear day with a fair wind, Leif hoisted sail and pointed his vessel westward. It was not a long run across Davis Strait, and Bjarni was able to advise him on the currents. Apparently he retraced Bjarni's voyage in reverse, for the Greenland Saga says:

> The first landfall they made was the country that Bjarni had sighted last. They sailed right up to the shore and cast anchor, then lowered a boat and landed. There was no grass to be seen, and the hinterland was covered with great glaciers, and between glaciers and shore the land was like one great slab of rock. It seemed to them a worthless country.
>
> Then Leif said, "Now we have done better than Bjarni where this country is concerned—we at least have set foot on it: I shall give this country a name and call it *Helluland* [Flat Rock Land]."

Where was Helluland? For that matter, where precisely were the other places that Leif visited? It is certain that they were on the coast of North America. But authorities disagree widely on the exact location. Some say Leif never got south of Newfoundland. Others say he reached Cape Cod. Still others have him venturing as far as Chesapeake Bay and even Florida.

Quite possibly Helluland was on the coast of Labrador. One can assume so from the description of ice mountains and from the fact that Leif was sailing before a northeast wind that, with the Labrador Current, likely could have carried him to this rocky, wintry shore. From this point, the saga continues:

> They returned to their ship and put to sea, and sighted a second land. Once again they sailed right up to it and cast anchor, lowered a boat and went ashore. This country was flat and wooded, with white sandy beaches wherever they went; and the land sloped gently down to the sea.
> Leif said, "This country shall be named after its natural resources: it shall be called *Markland* [Forest Land]."

From the description "flat and wooded" one might guess that this was Newfoundland or possibly even Nova Scotia, which is farther south than Newfoundland. Which land it actually was depends on how hard the northeast wind was blowing and how faithfully Leif followed the southward flowing current. The men did not tarry long at Markland. They were anxious to take advantage of the favorable wind, and they put to sea and sailed two more days.

Then they sighted a third land, and came ashore on an island of sweet-tasting grasses. From there they crossed an intervening sound and reached the mainland, poling their ship up a river and anchoring at an inland lake. They decided to spend the winter here, and they built "some large houses." It seemed like a gentle and promising land, with plenty of fish in lake and river and plenty of pastureland for livestock. "There was never any frost all winter and the grass hardly withered at all." The saga also says:

In this country, night and day were of more even length than in either Greenland or Iceland: on the shortest day of the year, the sun was already up by 9 A.M., and did not set until after 3 P.M.

From that statement one can judge that Leif's winter haven was somewhere between the Gulf of St. Lawrence and New Jersey. That is a large area, and two likely spots within it have been suggested as Leif's winter camp. One at its northernmost limit is Trinity Bay in Newfoundland. Another toward its southern limit is Cape Cod, with Nantucket the island of sweet grasses.

Leif now divided his company into two parties. One group spent each day exploring, the other tended to the houses and the need for food. Leif's foster father Tyrkir, who was with the exploring party, separated from his companions one day and disappeared. Leif upbraided his men for losing track of Tyrkir and launched a searching party.

They had gone only a short distance from the houses when Tyrkir came walking towards them, and they gave him a warm welcome.

Leif said to him, "Why are you so late, foster-father? How did you get separated from your companions?" . . .

"I did not go much farther than you," he [Tyrkir] said. "I have some news. I found vines and grapes."

"Is that true, foster-father?" asked Leif.

"Of course it is true," he replied. "Where I was born there were plenty of vines and grapes."

What can be learned of Leif's location from Tyrkir's discovery of vines and grapes? Not very much because in those years of generally warmer climate wild grapes were known to grow as far north as Newfoundland. And certainly they would be found anywhere in New England.

For Leif and his men, however, the discovery meant a valuable cargo to take home. Grape vines made excellent binding for the planks of Viking ships, and they also could be twisted into ropes and hawsers. The grapes themselves could be used for wine or they could be dried for raisins.

. . . Leif said to his men, "Now we have two tasks on our hands. On alternate days we must gather grapes and cut vines, and then fell trees, to make a cargo for my ship."

This was done. It is said that the tow-boat was filled with grapes. They took on a full cargo of timber; and in the spring they made ready to leave and sailed away. Leif named the country after its natural qualities and called it Vinland, [Vineland].

They put out to sea and had favourable winds all the way until they sighted Greenland and its ice-capped mountains.

Leif had one more adventure before reaching shore. He came upon a merchant vessel grounded on an offshore reef, and rescued all 15 of its crew. In return, he appropriated the ship's cargo and was able to sell it in Greenland at a healthy profit. This, with his own cargo of vines and lumber, made Leif a "wealthy and honorable man." It also gained him the title of "Leif the Lucky." This is perhaps unfair. For Leif had left nothing to fortune. He had set out to discover a new world, which Bjarni had sighted only from a distance, and with perseverance, skillful navigation, and good judgment he deservedly achieved his goal.

18

Thorvald Sails to His Death

It may seem strange that, having discovered a whole new world, Leif Ericsson never returned to Vinland. In fact, he scarcely went to sea again.

But there were sound reasons for this. Shortly after Leif's return, Eric the Red died. Leif inherited his father's position as Greenland's foremost chieftain, with all its homebound duties and responsibilities. He now had to concern himself with the welfare of Greenland, not with exploring other countries.

He could not, however, suppress the keen public interest that his western discoveries had aroused. Vinland became known as "Vinland the Good"—a paradise of verdant lands and gentle sunshine. Leif's younger brother Thorvald, in particular, wanted to visit the country, for he felt that Leif had not thoroughly explored it, and of course he was right. No one could thoroughly explore it in so short a time.

Leif agreed to lend Thorvald his ship, and it is recorded in the sagas that:

> Thorvald prepared his expedition with his brother Leif's guidance and engaged a crew of thirty. When the ship was ready they put out to sea and there are no reports of their voyage until they reached Leif's Houses in Vinland. There they laid up the ship and settled down for the winter, catching fish for their food.

Obviously, from this brief account, they had no trouble reaching Vinland. Doubtless some of the men in Thorvald's crew had been with Leif on his earlier voyage and knew precisely the course Leif had taken and where his shelters were.

In the spring Thorvald divided his men into two companies, leaving one to care for the ship and the shelters and to gather food for the following winter. The other group he took with him to explore the land to the west. For this pursuit they used the afterboat, which was carried on the ship's deck, for it was shallower and could easily be rowed up rivers or carried around obstacles.

They found "pleasing, well-wooded country, with the woods near the salt water and the white sands. There were many islands and shoals." If one accepts the theory that Leif's shelters were on Cape Cod, then the mention of "many islands and shoals" suggests the nearby New England coast of Massachusetts and Rhode Island. Again, one must remember that some authorities place Leif's camp as far to the north as Newfoundland.

The following summer Thorvald set out to explore to the north and east. This meant sailing in the open ocean, and the party shortly ran into a severe storm. The ship was driven ashore on a cape; and, although no men were lost, the keel was badly damaged and had to be replaced.

It is not hard to imagine what a difficult, time-consuming job this was. The ship had to be unloaded and rolled up on shore over logs. Temporary shelters had to be constructed for the men. Then the forests had to be searched for a straight oak that would yield a beam exactly the size of the damaged keel. This had to be shaped and trimmed, the old keel pried loose from the hull, and the new keel put in its place. The entire hull no doubt had to be caulked anew, with resin from the forest trees.

Thorvald ordered the old keel to be erected at the end of the cape as a marker, and gave this spit of land the name Keelness, or Keel Cape. If only that piece of oak or parts of it preserved in the sand and clay could be found today, historians would know a good deal more about the Vikings' Vinland explorations.

With the ship repaired, Thorvald continued to sail north and east. He kept well out to sea to avoid the reefs and rocky islands of the coast line. Eventually he came to a steep fjord reminiscent of the fjords of Norway. It was surrounded by wooded cliffs and mountains. Since they were still "far out at sea" when they discovered it, one could assume that this fjord was Somes Sound in Mount Desert Island, Maine. Certainly this place fits the description better than any other fjord in North America, although at least one other Viking authority identifies Thorvald's fjord as Hamilton Inlet on the coast of Labrador.

They moored their ship inside the fjord, and Thorvald and his men went ashore and climbed to higher ground to look around.

"It is beautiful here," said Thorvald. "This is where I would like to make my home." For a Viking to want to settle for good on any spot was a sure sign that he was pleased with what he saw.

On their way back to the ship the group was surprised to see three overturned skin boats, or hide-covered canoes, on a strip of sand. They went over to investigate and were still more surprised to find that each boat sheltered a sleeping Indian, or *skraeling* as the Vikings called them.

This was the first encounter between a European man and an American Indian, and unfortunately it set the pattern of following encounters through a thousand years of history. Both sides were startled and distrustful and inevitably someone panicked. The Indians tried to rush their boats into the water, and all but one were killed in their battle to escape. The survivor paddled frantically up the fjord and disappeared.

Disturbed by the presence of the Indians, Thorvald led his men to the crest of a nearby mountain from which they could survey the surrounding countryside. They could see

no sign of the escaping skraeling and his boat, but they did detect what might have been an Indian encampment farther up the fjord. When they returned to the shore where their ship was anchored, Thorvald was careful to appoint a sentry to stand guard over his sleeping men throughout the night.

Sometime during the early morning, the warning cry sounded: "Wake up, Thorvald, and all you men! If you would save yourselves, go to the ship with all speed and get clear of land!"

The warning had come just in time. The aroused men saw a whole tribe of Indians approaching swiftly in canoes, and the Greenlanders barely had time to reach the safety of the ship. But there was no time to hoist sail and escape. They rowed the ship out from shore, and Thorvald ordered shields to be hung on the gunwale to deflect the rain of arrows that now descended on them.

It was fortunate that the Viking ships were made of stalwart oak and that the barrier of shields had been provided. Otherwise the Indians might have exacted bloody vengeance for their slaughtered comrades. As it was, most of the arrows shattered harmlessly against the shields and stout sides of the knorr. The Indians did not try to board the ship. The sight of the helmeted Vikings with unfamiliar swords and axes warned them to keep their distance and, having spent their arrows, they finally retreated up the fjord.

Thorvald asked if any of his men were wounded. Assured that none was, he told them:

"I have a wound beneath my arm. An arrow flew between the side of the ship and the shield and struck me. Here it is. This will lead to my death. Bury me on that piece of land I thought so lovely for a home. For it seems I spoke the truth when I said that I would dwell here for a while."

The men did as Thorvald asked. He found his permanent home in Vinland. When the ship and its crew returned to Greenland, with a cargo of grapes and vines, "they had much to tell Leif Ericsson."

By now two of Eric's sons, Thorvald and Leif, had visited Vinland, leaving only the youngest son, Thorstein, to have missed the great adventure of the Viking age. Thorstein must have felt like a grounded astronaut whose brothers had already reached the moon. He was compelled to make the trip himself. Using the excuse that he wanted to avenge Thorvald's death, or at least recover Thorvald's body, he fitted out the same ship and set sail with his wife for Vinland with a hastily recruited crew.

Thorstein's voyage can be summarized in a single sentence from the sagas: "Throughout that summer they were at the mercy of the weather and never knew where they were going."

Quite evidently Thorstein was not the able navigator that his father and brothers were. After thrashing hopelessly about the sea lanes west of Greenland, storm tossed and wind driven, running low on water and supplies, his party found itself forced to land on the barren northwest shore of Greenland. It was then October, too late to try to sail for home.

Thorstein turned the ship over to his crew as living quarters, and he and his wife found shelter at the farm of a minor chieftain in the neighborhood. There Thorstein was stricken by the plague and died. The expedition achieved one distinction. It was perhaps the most futile voyage in Viking history.

19

The Viking Dream Ends

It was more than 15 years now since Vinland had been discovered and explored by Eric's sons. It had become the Promised Land to adventurous Vikings ploughing western seas. Yet no one had tried to settle there or establish a permanent colony in North America. The time was ripe for such an attempt, for unclaimed land was growing scarce in Greenland and in other Viking countries.

About the year 1010 (the sagas fail to give exact dates) a man named Thorfin Karlsefni arrived at Ericsfjord from Iceland. Though still quite young, Karlsefni was a wealthy seagoing trader and a man of noble birth, a descendant of the famous Ragnar Lodbrok. Karlsefni's ship was accompanied by a second vessel commanded by a man named Bjarni Grimolfsson. Each ship carried 40 men, many looking for land to settle on in Greenland.

Karlsefni was heartily welcomed by Leif at Ericsfjord. Gifts were exchanged, the trading went smoothly, and finally Leif invited the Icelanders to spend the winter at Brattalid. Since it was late in the autumn and there was plenty of room, the visitors readily accepted.

Christmas was celebrated with a lavish banquet in the great hall, with flaming yule log and special foods that Thorfin Karlsefni had brought from Iceland. During and after these festivities Karlsefni courted Gudrid, Thorstein's widow, and asked Leif for her hand. Leif and Gudrid agreed to the marriage, which took place after New Year's.

The sagas relate that "there was great good cheer at Brattalid that winter, with gaming and storytelling and similar things which contributed to the entertainment of the household." Certainly much of the storytelling concerned the discovery of Vinland, which had captured everyone's imagination. Even Gudrid was still eager to explore this wonderful new country. Perhaps she and Karlsefni would make their home there.

Before the winter months were over, plans had been made to visit Vinland that summer—not simply to explore the country but to settle there "if they were strong enough."

Altogether, four ships were outfitted for the expedition. There were the two that Karlsefni and Bjarni had brought from Iceland. Of the other two, one was captained by a Viking named Thorhall the Hunter who was overseer of Leif Ericsson's estate, the other by Leif's brother-in-law

Thorvard, husband of Leif's sister Freydis Ericsdottir.

The fleet carried 160 people, about 40 to a ship, including women and children. In addition, the heavily loaded vessels carried food and water for the company and cattle with which to start farming in the new land. Among the cattle was a "rambunctious bull" which, besides being hard to handle aboard the ship, played an unforeseen role in the adventure.

Three different sagas tell of Karlsefni's voyage, and no two agree precisely. The three accounts are the *Thorfin Karlsefni Saga*, *Eric the Red Saga*, and the *Greenlander's Story* or Flaytebok. The best that one can do is to compare the three and combine those parts of each that seem best to fit the circumstances.

Karlsefni's vessel was the leader of the fleet. Wary of what had befallen Thorstein Ericsson, and feeling responsible for the women and children in the overloaded ships, Karlsefni took the safest route. He led the ships north up the Greenland coast to just opposite Baffin Island, and crossed over where Davis Strait is narrowest, never being out of sight of land for long. He then led his small fleet south down the Labrador coast, aided by the southbound current, and passed Helluland and Markland, which Leif had told him about.

When he came to Keel Cape, where Thorvald had left his damaged keel as a marker, he knew he was on the right course. But he still did not know where Vinland lay. He supposed it must be farther south and kept on in that direction. At one point two scouts were sent ashore and returned with handfuls of "wineberries and self-sown wheat," persuading Karlsefni that he was not far from Vinland.

At length the ships came to a fjord with strong down currents. They named this Straumfjord, or Stream Fjord, and here they landed. It was late summer now, and they carried their cargoes ashore and planned to winter there. They built a series of one-room houses of turf and stone a little up from shore, and here Karlsefni's son Snorri was born to Gudrid—the first European born in North America.

As recently as 1963 a Norwegian scholar named Helge Instad discovered the remains of a Norse camp at L'Anse aux Meadows on Epaves Bay on the northern peninsula of Newfoundland. If this was the site of Karlsefni's winter quarters, the first European settlement in the New World, then Straumfjord must have been the Labrador Current flowing through this strait.

The winter was hard on the settlers at Straumfjord and they prayed for food. Thorhall the Hunter, being pagan, composed a special appeal to the Viking god Thor, and almost immediately a whale was stranded on the beach below the camp. The company stuffed themselves on whale meat until Thorhall informed them that the whale was an answer to his prayer to Thor. Whereupon the Christian Icelanders are said to have developed violent stomachaches and dumped the remainder of the whale meat into the sea.

Possibly because of this rebuke to his religious beliefs,

Thorhall decided to leave the company. Perhaps, too, he thought that Vinland lay farther north, for he sailed away in that direction. He was caught in a storm and driven east clear to Ireland. Here his ship and company were captured, the men enslaved, and Thorhall killed.

When spring came to Straumfjord, Karlsefni reloaded the three remaining ships and traveled south along the coast.

> They sailed for a long time and eventually came to a river that flowed down into a lake and from the lake into the sea. There were extensive sandbars outside the river mouth, and ships could only enter it at high tide.
>
> Karlsefni and his men sailed into the estuary and named the place *Hope* [Tidal Lake]. Here they found wild wheat growing in fields on all the low ground and grape vines on all the higher ground. Every stream was teeming with fish. They dug trenches at the high-tide mark, and when the tide went out there were halibut trapped in the trenches. In the woods there was a great number of animals of all kinds.

Whether or not this was Vinland, Karlsefni found it promising. People went ashore and took their cattle, and they started to build shelters on the sloping lakeside. But in two weeks' time they encountered what they had dreaded: Indians.

The skraelings came in "a great number of skin boats," holloing and brandishing what looked like weapons. Wisely,

Karlsefni greeted them in friendly fashion, displaying a white shield to denote peace. The Indians seemed only curious. The Vikings indicated in sign language that they had articles to trade for furs and walrus hides and anything else the Indians might have to offer. On this promising note, the Indians sailed off to the south and disappeared.

This first peaceful meeting with the Indians assured the Vikings that it would be safe to remain at Hope for the winter, which they did. Eric's saga notes, "There was no snow at all, and all the livestock were able to fend for themselves [live by grazing]."

This comment on the weather might be a clue to Hope's location. However, the various sagas often contradict each other. What is more, various modern scholars who have studied these sagas interpret them differently. One scholar says, for example, that Straumfjord was the Hudson River and Hope was the mouth of Chesapeake Bay. On the other hand, those who believe that Karlsefni's first quarters were on Epaves Bay place Hope farther south on the Newfoundland peninsula.

Early in the spring, after a winter spent hovering around the fires in their sod huts, Karlsefni's people sighted "a great horde of skin boats approaching from the south. It looked as if the estuary were strewn with charcoal." The Indians in every boat were waving staves, and the Vikings grabbed their swords and shields. But it soon became apparent that the natives had come to trade, not fight.

Among other things, the Indians coveted the red wool

which the Vikings wore and which they used to mend their sails. For this the Indians were willing to exchange far more precious furs and hides. The skraelings also wanted weapons, which Karlsefni wisely denied them. Shrewd in the art of trading, Karlsefni had the wool cloth cut up into narrow strips, demanding a heavy price in furs for each abbreviated piece.

As the trading was proceeding smoothly there occurred one of those chance incidents that bring on catastrophe. The rambunctious bull, which was grazing with the Viking cattle, for some strange reason became enraged at the sight of the skraelings. The bull charged toward them from the pasture, snorting violently.

Panic seized the Indians. They had never seen an animal like this. Some of them fled frantically to their canoes. Others tried to enter the houses for protection. The Vikings thought that the Indians had treacherously started to attack. Brandishing swords and axes the Norsemen forced the skraelings from the buildings and drove them to their boats. The Indians rowed away furiously, leaving their bundles of furs and cloth behind them.

Unwittingly the Vikings—or more specifically the truculent bull—had changed the friendly Indians into sworn enemies. Karlsefni felt sure they would return to get revenge and repossess their bundles. He told his men:

"This is what we must do: ten men are to go out on the headland here and make themselves conspicuous, and the rest of us are to go into the wood and make a clearing there, where we can keep our cattle when the Skraelings come out of the forest. We shall take our bull and keep him to the fore."

Karlsefni was right about the Indians returning. Three weeks later they arrived in force, waving sticks and slings as they stormed the beach. Karlsefni's men emerged from their ambush and clashed with the invaders. The sagas do not say what happened to the bull in the ensuing battle.

Among their weapons the Indians had a type of sling that discharged a rock wrapped in animal skin. It made a frightening noise as it whirled toward its target.

The Vikings were not used to flying missiles. They preferred hand-to-hand combat with swords and axes. As arrows and stones poured into their ranks, they fled in terror to the woods. It was a single woman who held her ground. She was Eric's daughter Freydis. Freydis snatched up a sword and waved it threateningly at the Indians. A woman warrior, like the charging bull, was such an unfamiliar sight that the skraelings raced to their boats and fled, leaving two Vikings slain and four of their own dead.

Karlsefni and his men sheepishly congratulated Freydis on her bravery; she had proved to be the mightiest Viking of them all. But they knew now that they were living in jeopardy. Vinland, America, could not be colonized so long as the Indians had them hopelessly outnumbered. The Vikings, of course, had only themselves to blame for the hostility of the Indian people. Just so, the European settlers of later generations were to incur the wrath of the much-abused American Indian.

Planning now to return to Greenland, Karlsefni loaded up the boats with vines and lumber. The Vikings then sailed north on a favorable wind. As they passed Markland they came ashore for water and encountered five more Indians, three adults and two boys. As the parents fled, the Vikings captured the children and resolved to take them home as slaves. Then they crossed east to Greenland and came to rest at Ericsfjord.

However, of the three remaining ships, one did not make it back to Greenland. Bjarni Grimolfsson became separated from the others, and his worm-eaten vessel began to sink. Some of his men escaped in their afterboat and finally reached Greenland safely. But Bjarni gave up his place in the lifeboat to a fellow Viking and perished at sea.

There is a dubious footnote to this chapter of Viking history. It concerns Eric's daughter Freydis. One saga relates that Freydis and her company remained at Straumfjord when the others left. Another saga says she later made a separate voyage to Vinland. But both accounts report that Freydis' company fell to quarreling among each other and that the ferocious Freydis herself slew the opposing Vikings as they slept, returning to Greenland with the rest. Evidently Leif learned of Freydis' villainy. But since she was his sister he did nothing about it, only prophesying that "she will not prosper from this act."

Thus, somewhat ingloriously, ended the Vikings' attempt to colonize North America—leaving that effort to the Spanish, French, and English colonists who followed five centuries later.

~~~~~~~~~~~~~~~~~~~~~~~~~~~~~~~~~~~~

By 1066, the year of the Norman invasion of England, the great Viking days were all but over. History gives the year 1100 as the end of the Viking era. By then the seaborne warriors had become settled citizens of many countries. They had put aside the sword in favor of the plow, had replaced the warship with the merchant knorr. They had cast off the pagan gods and become generally peaceful Christians. Never again would they range abroad, in great force, seeking forbidden wealth or lands to conquer.

What had happened? Why did they change?

Many things had happened, and some the Vikings brought upon themselves. Their ruthless raids had forced neighboring countries to strengthen defenses on land and sea. Plunder and conquest became increasingly difficult, and then almost impossible, without the risk of serious defeat.

In Scandinavian mythology the term *Ragnarok*, or Twilight of the Gods, applies to "the destruction of the gods and all things in a great battle with evil powers." In keeping with their beliefs the Vikings apparently felt that their world would end in a mighty battle and, appropriately, they would go down fighting. Ironically it was the forces of peace and civilization that finally overwhelmed them.

For one thing, they discovered, or decided, that trade was more lucrative than war. With trading ports established in the countries they had colonized or conquered, it was easier to get what they wanted in exchange for their furs and hides and slaves than to seize it by force. Even countries as remote and detached from the Viking world as Arabia and the Orient were glad to do business with Viking fleets of ships and caravans.

By association with the countries that they traded with or had conquered, the Vikings themselves became more civilized. They had acquired many of the luxuries of living of that time; there were no longer things that they desperately wanted. Life had become more comfortable and more bountiful, and they were more content. The Vikings had not been defeated, simply tamed.

They had also mixed and married with so many different peoples—Irish, English, Russian, French, and Greek—that they no longer could regard these people as potential enemies or victims.

What, then, had all their voyages and adventures amounted to? Some say that the Vikings swept into world history and out again like a mighty windstorm, leaving behind temporary wreckage and not much else. But consider these points:

From Viking times until today, the great trade routes of the world are those that were established by the Vikings.

The people of medieval Europe were jolted out of their Dark Age lethargy. Europeans and others who rose against the Viking threat found new strength and purpose. Divided nations were eventually united against the common enemy.

The Vikings' discovery of the New World was like man's landing on the moon. It may have led to no immediate benefit to mankind, but it proved what men could achieve with combined skills, courage, and imagination.

The Vikings' mastery of shipbuilding and naval architecture led other nations such as England to attempt to equal their high standard. This contributed to the eventual construction of the great navies and merchant fleets that made history on the North Atlantic.

Institutions such as the Icelandic Althing were patterns for future, rising democracies. Viking sagas created a distinct new literature for future generations. And by their own conversion and overseas migrations, the Vikings extended the spread of Christianity and other civilizing influences around the world.

Finally, a measure of Viking blood and Viking character has descended to many modern peoples. Perhaps that is one reason why modern man is so restless and so eager to improve his lot. So long as new frontiers remain, in the oceans and in space, man will not be content until he has conquered them.

Selected Further Reading

BRØGGER, A. W., and SHETELIG, H., *The Viking Ships*. Oslo, K. K. Morgensen, 1953. Complete description, with photographs and diagrams, of Viking ships and how they were built.

BRØNDSTED, JOHANNES, *The Vikings*. Baltimore, Penguin (paperback), 1965. A short account of the Viking era, with chapters on Viking towns and camps, runic inscriptions, and the Viking way of life. With photographs.

Donovan, F. R., *The Vikings*. New York, American Heritage (a Horizon Book), 1964. Abundantly illustrated history, with drawings, maps, and photographs.

Hendrick, T. D., *A History of the Vikings*. New York, Barnes & Noble, 1930. A detailed and somewhat technical textbook, with maps and photographs.

Janeway, Elizabeth, *The Vikings*. New York, Random House (a Landmark Book), 1951. Partially fictionalized account of the Viking voyages to America, for younger readers.

Jones, Gwyn, *A History of the Vikings*. New York, Oxford University Press, 1968. Very thorough and comprehensive, with maps, diagrams, and photographs.

MAGNUSSON, M., and PALSSON, H., *The Vinland Sagas*. New York, New York University Press, 1966. Translations of the Greenland Saga and Eric the Red Saga, covering Viking voyages to America.

Mowat, Farley, *Westviking*. Boston, Little, Brown, 1965. Concentrates on Norse voyages to Greenland and America, with maps.

Newman, Robert, *Grettir the Strong*. New York, Thomas Y. Crowell, 1968. Presents one of the more famous Icelandic sagas in freely translated form.

Pohl, F. J., *The Viking Explorers*. New York, Thomas Y. Crowell, 1966. Text, photographs, and many maps document the author's claim for Viking landings in America far south of New England.

Sawyer, P. H., *The Age of the Vikings*. New York, St. Martin's Press, 1962. Surveys how the Vikings lived, their homes, their customs, their ships, and their settlements.

Simpson, Jacqueline, *Everyday Life in the Viking Age*. New York, Putnam's, 1967. Portrays the character of the Vikings; how they lived, played, and worked. Illustrated.

Index

ABOUT THE AUTHOR

Samuel Carter III has always been interested in sailing and has cruised the North Atlantic coast, visiting many of the places where the Vikings are said to have landed. A trip to Scandinavia and especially the Viking museums at Oslo and Stockholm reenforced his interest in these extraordinary people.

Mr. Carter was graduated from Princeton and Oxford and studied at the Sorbonne in Paris for a year. Then he traveled to Spain where he was trapped in Barcelona by the Spanish Civil War. On his return he wrote articles and stories about this experience and he has been writing ever since. He has worked in radio, television, and the movies, and has had short stories and articles published in many leading magazines. Among his books are *How to Sail*, *Kingdom of the Tides*, *The Gulf Stream Story*, *Lightning Beneath the Sea*, *The Incredible Great White Fleet*, *The Happy Dolphins*, and *Blaze of Glory: The Fight for New Orleans*. Mr. Carter's hobbies are sailing, flying, and skin-diving. He now lives in Connecticut, but he has a pair of "adopted" dolphins in Florida which he tries to spend some time with each winter.

ABOUT THE ILLUSTRATOR

Ted Burwell studied at the Newark School of Fine and Industrial Art in New Jersey and at the School of Visual Arts in New York, where he received awards in painting. He currently employs his talent as book designer and production editor for major publishing houses. His free time is spent playing jazz guitar, listening to jazz—and illustrating books.

Mr. Burwell particularly "enjoys doing any job with an historic background and the ensuing research into the customs, artifacts, and costumes of a given period." VIKINGS BOLD, he tells us, "offered an excellent opportunity to capture the unique flavor of a period and give the feeling of really living in it."

Ted Burwell lives with his wife and two daughters in Hillside, New Jersey.